Leading Standards-Based Education Reform

Improving Implementation of Standards to Increase Student Achievement

Linda R. Vogel

ROWMAN & LITTLEFIELD EDUCATION
A division of
ROWMAN & LITTLEFIELD PUBLISHERS, INC.
Lanham • New York • Toronto • Plymouth, UK

Published by Rowman & Littlefield Education
A division of Rowman & Littlefield Publishers, Inc.
A wholly owned subsidary of The Rowman & Littlefield Publishing Group, Inc.
4501 Forbes Boulevard, Suite 200, Lanham, Maryland 20706
http://www.rowmaneducation.com

Estover Road, Plymouth PL6 7PY, United Kingdom

British Library Cataloguing in Publication Information Available

Library of Congress Cataloging in Publication Data

Vogel, Linda R.
  Leading standards based education reform : improving implementation of
standards to increase student achievement / Linda R. Vogel.
     p.   cm.
  Includes bibliographical references.
  ISBN 978 1 60709 981 9 (cloth : alk. paper)   ISBN 978 1 60709 982 6
(pbk. : alk. paper)   ISBN 978 1 60709 983 3 (electronic)
  1. Education   Standards   United States   Handbooks, manuals, etc. 2.
Educational accountability   United States   Handbooks, manuals, etc. 3.
Educational evaluation   United States   Handbooks, manuals, etc. I. Title.
  LB3060.83.V65 2010
  379.1' 580973   dc22   2010029029

♾ The paper used in this publication meets the minimum requirements of
American National Standard for Information Sciences   Permanence of
Paper for Printed Library Materials, ANSI/NISO Z39.48 1992.

Printed in the United States of America

Contents

Preface

In teaching educational leadership classes at the university level and as a former principal, I have read literally hundreds of books and articles that lay out a list of what one needs to do to be an effective leader and how to navigate or instigate change or reform America s public schools. I prefer the approach of Michael Fullan, who makes observations and stresses that one must act in accordance with the specific context of your own organi zation and situation.

The steps in each stage described in this book are intended as guides based on the observed actions and results of educators in eight unique school districts, not as a rigid prescription that will be a silver bullet in every district or school.

While the challenges of closing the achievement gap and making the most of resources faced each of the districts observed and are common in schools across America, the guidance contained in the following chapters must be applied with an acute mindfulness of your district s and school s unique cultural, economic, and political context. Replication of results is never as simple as following a predefined to do list because no group of people or community is the same.

This book does describe essential communications, investments in re sources, and the development of structures that support and can advance individual and organizational learning and change in using educational standards to support student engagement and learning. As with any re source, it is to be used to prompt discussion and exploration of alterna tives to current practice for the enrichment of student learning experiences and increased student achievement.

Chapter One

Standards, Accountability, and Leadership

The fundamental question that needs to be asked of any reform initia
tive is, Does it change classroom instruction and improve the learning
opportunities and outcomes for all students?

Nearly a decade after the passage of the No Child Left Behind (NCLB)
reauthorization of the Elementary and Secondary School Act (2001), it
would be difficult to find a public school in the forty nine states across
America where the teachers and administrators would say that the curricu
lum they teach is *not* standards based.[1] Bolstered by the requirement for
Adequate Yearly Progress (AYP) of students across racial and socioeco
nomic groups in reading, writing, and mathematics, state accountability
systems have been created and strengthened to monitor the progress of
schools in helping all students reach a level of proficiency in these core
skill and subject areas.

For public schools to continue to receive state and federal funding,
meeting accountability goals is a mandate, not an option. The path that
each district and school takes in pursuit of the goal of educating all stu
dents to a level of state defined proficiency differs, depending on the
philosophy, resources, and demographic makeup of each educational
community. The results of each district s and schools efforts differ as
well, as unique educational philosophies guide the selection and alloca
tion of resources deemed appropriate or adequate to meet the needs of the
students served.

How schools and teachers implement standards based education is very
dependent on district and school leaders. This book examines the efforts

1

of administrators and teachers in eight school districts in a Rocky Moun
tain state, varying in size and resources but all facing the common chal
lenge of helping their students achieve proficiency on state assessments
of learning standards.

School systems are loosely coupled (Weick 1976), meaning that man
dates and reforms are interpreted and morph as they are implemented.
On the positive side, this has sometimes allowed good teaching to persist
despite poor leadership. It often also means that the best intentions of
administrators do not always translate into positive changes in teaching
or student learning. Unintended consequences and versions of mandates
and reform efforts abound in the history of public school reform (Fullan
2001a).

As accountability stakes heighten, it becomes essential for administra
tors and teachers to have a common working understanding of what is ex
pected, both of teachers and students, and the appropriate tools to be used
to reach common goals of student learning. This book explains the four
stages of standards based education implementation identified from the
experiences of the eight school districts studied, highlighting the actions,
support, and training in each stage that helped administrators and teach
ers positively change both their philosophy and their practice in teaching
students and supporting student achievement.

While standards and the related accountability systems have been both
praised and criticized by educators, it is important to understand the value
and the pitfalls of each to truly appreciate the environment of change and
challenge that educators in the twenty first century era of NCLB face.
This chapter provides a brief history and a summary of both the praise
and the criticism of standards and accountability systems as well as how
district and school leadership is essential to gleaning the best of both to
support effective teaching and student learning.

A BRIEF HISTORY OF EDUCATIONAL STANDARDS

The National Commission on Excellence in Education (NCEE) announced
the crisis in public education in their 1983 report *A Nation at Risk.* At the
end of the Cold War and the beginning of truly global economic competi

tion, America was perceived as losing its competitive edge. When evalu ated by President Reagan s blue ribbon panel, the NCEE, education was identified as a major breach in the nation s ability to respond to rapidly changing markets in the global arena.

In what has become an infamous indictment of American public educa tion, the NCEE report stated that a rising tide of mediocrity that threatens our very future as a nation and a people (National Commission on Excel lence in Education 1983, 1) existed in public schools as a result of poor teaching, likening the crisis to unilateral disarmament in the economic war for markets with other industrial nations whose students outper formed ours on international mathematics and literacy tests (Foorman, Kalinowski, and Sexton 2007, 20). In response to the educational crisis heralded by the NCEE report, states responded with a variety of reform initiatives, including learning standards.

In *Governing Public Schools: New Times, New Requirements*, Danz berger, Kirst, and Usdan (1992) describe numerous efforts of governors, legislators, and businessmen to initiate education reform measures. They explained that implicitly or explicitly many outside reformers see the educational establishment as being part of the problem of the nation s educational crisis. That is one reason why governors, their education aides, and state legislators have joined business leaders in seizing the initiative in educational policy making all over the country. . . . These pressures may lead to even more radical reforms at the national level such as the development of national assessments or standards that may well drive the curriculum in our heretofore decentralized educational gover nance system (7). Efforts to respond to this national crisis included the National Educational Goals Panel, the National Council for Educational Standards and Testing, the New Standards Project, the National Assess ment of Educational Progress, and the U.S. Labor Department Secretary s Commission on Achieving Necessary Skills in the workplace.

Although many educators pointed out weaknesses in the premise of this education crisis based on international test scores (Berliner and Biddle 1996; Bracey 2004), few could disagree that the achievement gap between racial and socioeconomic groups of students did not exist and had seri ous implications for those students who were underachieving as well as society as a whole.

While many states developed broad educational goals and required school districts to also develop a variety of learning objectives throughout the late 1980s and early 1990s, it was not until the late 1990s that states began to adopt learning standards and related benchmarks. Early efforts received mixed reviews from educators, in part because the mandates did originate from groups outside of education, even though educators were usually included in the actual development of the goals and, later, standards.

Until states began to implement accountability systems to monitor stu dent achievement of standards, learning goals and objectives developed at the local level often became shelf documents that had little influence on curriculum or instructional methods let alone student learning.

The National Council for Teachers of Mathematics (NCTM) had de veloped widely recognized, useful standards during the 1980s, and this teacher led effort provided hope in the development of standards in other content areas. Linda Darling Hammond (1997) discussed the merits of standards, using the NCTM standards as an example, as being clear enough to help teachers develop curricula pointed in a common direction, but they are not so voluminous and prescriptive as to require superficial content coverage or to limit teachings inventiveness in bringing ideas to life for students (227).

By illuminating the structure of the discipline and the goals of teach ing and learning (Darling Hammond 1997, 227), standards can provide guideposts for teachers who could then, in turn, tailor curriculum to build on individual student interests and needs.

AN IMPERFECT ROAD MAP

There are few educators who would disagree with Darling Hammond s (1997) assessment that a coherent view of curriculum, assessment, and teaching is at the core of any vision of more effective education. Educa tion standards have become the major policy vehicle in part because they can reflect changes in goals, including, for example, the major shift in the kind of learning our society desires of young people, which in turn requires a major shift in teaching and schooling. . . . Depending on how they are fashioned and used, however, standards for learning can either energize or kill reform (211). The crux of the matter is how standards are fashioned and how they are used in accountability systems, and therein lays the root of the love/hate relationship many educators have with learn ing standards.

A number of educators and education critics point out that standards can inhibit teachers creativity to tailor instruction to spark the interest and motivation of students, to make content relevant to students life situations, and to spend the appropriate amount of time and activity in a classroom to ensure a deep understanding of significant concepts (Kohn 1999; Meier 2000; Ohanian 1999). Standards can be written in such detail that they inhibit the inclusion of other material that local educators deem significant and relevant to students or standards can be written so vaguely that they give little guidance to educators.

Many books have been written and professional development semi nars provided to assist educators in using standards in a meaningful way, whether they are written too broadly or too narrowly (Reeves 2002, 2003; Ainsworth 2003a, 2003b). A significant criticism leveled at standards based education is also the time taken away from other subjects that are measured by state accountability systems, with research identifying a 32 percent reduction in time spent teaching social studies, science, art, music, physical education, as well as lunch and recess (Mc Murrer 2007). This criticism and the correlating criticism that teachers teach to the test are actually consequences of accountability systems, not learning standards.

Despite these challenges and unintended consequences, state learning standards have provided both new and experienced teachers with common direction as to what to teach, no longer leaving it up to the local school or district to decide what should be taught and when. While some may lament this change as a decrease in local control of public education, new teachers particularly often appreciate the guidance.

A third year teacher in a small, rural district explained that in the few years that I have been teaching, I ve used the standards to guide instruc tion. Just to make sure that I have a road map and the students have a road map as to what they are going to be learning throughout the year so I just use them to guide instruction.

A sixth year math teacher described his first years as being guided by the textbooks he was given, but, I kind of made judgments on my own this is important at this age and this is not. The standards definitely focus you more. A more experienced teacher explained that he liked how the state s standards were written because it s not all inclusive and it s not limiting. But it does provide a base. . . . You know, education shouldn t be dependent on the individual preferences of a teacher or a principal and a student ought to be able to count on this quality of an education regardless of where they go to school at.

With teaching experience, standards may become more of a reference or reminder rather than a closely read road map. One science teacher nearing her twentieth year in teaching observed that if you re a good teacher, you re hitting the standards, no matter what. Another experi enced teacher felt that the standards were not just an influence now it is my instruction.

State learning standards also help administrators in eliminating redun dancy in the curriculum. As one small rural superintendent explained, When I first came here, I was appalled to see the curriculum and in struction that was in the district. There was no rhyme or reason of why we were doing some of the things that we were doing. He went on to explain that, through the curriculum mapping process, the second , third , and fourth grade teachers all discovered that they were teaching units on dinosaurs but not spending much time on math or fractions. The kids were getting overdosed in certain areas and very much under dosed in other areas.

The standards allowed him to bring the teachers together and make their own decisions on what would be taught at each grade level without his direct intervention. This valuable process of back mapping curricula from the desired outcomes of a twelfth grade public education would be much more laborious and incongruent without state learning standards. The motivation to undertake such work might also be nonexistent without state accountability systems.

More recently, efforts by the Council of Chief State School Officers and the National Governors Association to create national standards in the Common Core State Standards Initiative may be followed with the use of the National Assessment of Educational Progress (NAEP) to measure student progress and hold schools accountable at a federal level (Cava nagh 2010).

THE ACCOUNTABILITY STICK

While few, if any, educators purposefully set out *not* to teach the children under their care, the adoption of NCLB and resulting state accountability systems have definitely required educators to sit up and pay close attention to what students are learning. Educators are now personally responsible in a public venue with very real consequences attached to student performance on state examinations. Just as students may not relish taking assessments, it is how any assessment is used that really determines its value in accomplishing a behavioral or learning goal.

As an assistant superintendent of a large and progressive school dis trict explained, teachers used to have the perspective of I taught it. They didn t learn it. Not my problem. That attitude changed when a result of students not learning became school reorganization, a common consequence in many state accountability systems for low performing schools where teachers and school leaders are moved to another school or dismissed.

Educators, just like students, need and frequently appreciate knowing what they are being held accountable for and being able to demonstrate progress toward those goals. There must be the perception that progress can be made, however (Covington 1993; Rogers, Ludington, and Graham 1997). The frustrations that educators experience with state and federal accountability measures is that they feel that they lack the resources to compensate within the classroom or school for social and economic fac tors that influence students academic success.

As Rothstein (2004) bluntly states in his introductory section titled Good teachers, high expectations, standards, accountability, and inspi ration are not enough,   The influence of social class characteristics is probably so powerful that schools cannot overcome it, no matter how well trained their teachers and no matter how well designed are their instruc tional programs and climate (5).

NCLB is frequently the crux of these frustrations, with an array of complaints ranging from forcing schools to teach to the test and con straining the curriculum to punishing schools for having students who are English language learners, special education students, and students living in poverty.

Commenting on the effects of the state s assessment on his teaching, a science teacher in a poor, industrial urban school district vented that rather than educating students and using their knowledge and the way they can discover knowledge or use those skills whenever it comes up on the test, it s becoming skill and drill.

He went on to explain that the root of his frustration was NCLB and the AYP requirement: It s becoming more constraining as time goes on because they ratchet up with [the goal for] 2014 being 100%, everybody, being proficient which is impossible. You know that statistically it is impossible to reach that and I believe a lot of that legislation is designed to make public schools look bad, damage public education, and open the way for vouchers.

The challenge of providing compensatory education to students learn ing English as a second language or who have not been exposed to reading materials outside the schoolhouse, to name just a few of the intervening variables in education, remains daunting.

Recognizing the impact of a variety of factors that exist outside the educational arena, the Editorial Projects in Education Research Center (EPERC) developed a Chance for Success index. This index consid ers such factors as family income, parental education and employment, linguistic integration, preschool and kindergarten enrollment, adult edu cational attainment, annual income, and rate of employment to measure the progress of states in addressing factors related to student academic performance (Hightower 2010). The EPERC also assesses the financial resources allocated to schools in each state, recognizing that resources are unequal.

The expected outcomes are the same for all schools, regardless of resources, however. The observation that cows need to be fed, not just weighed is often linked to the inequity of resources schools have to draw on to address the many learning challenges of students across the socio economic spectrum.

Larry Cuban (2003) succinctly critiques the morally righteous NCLB call for all children to learn as only the beginning of the paragraph. The full paragraph should read: All children can learn *if* state legislatures provide schools with adequate funds, if all children are healthy and ready for school, if they have certified teachers earn ing adequate salaries, small class size, and sufficient time to learn according to their stages of intellectual and social development (43). Cuban goes on to discuss the need for an affirmative action version of equality that gives resources to students and schools to more ef fectively level the playing field of learning and academic achievement for minority and at risk students. The reality is, however, that resources are increasingly tight at both the federal and the local levels, and the mandate to increase student achievement remains, so consequences will be enacted despite the lack of appropriate support for low performing schools and students.

More recently, Rothstein et al. (2008) condemns the premise of ac countability based on test scores as having corrupted schools. Despite such criticisms, federal and state accountability systems have changed very little. There may be no carrot, but there definitely still is a stick.

LEADERSHIP REQUIRED

Despite the very real social challenges that educators face, most often without additional resources, a no excuses attitude has developed, par ticularly among administrators. To lead a school or district in the NCLB era, administrators have had to adopt the philosophy that they will do as much as they possibly can given whatever the circumstances of the school or students may be.

Leadership is definitely what is required to allocate resources and pro vide the training and support to teachers to identify and most effectively deal with the challenges inherent in increasing the demonstrated learning and achievement of all students despite the unlevel playing field created by social and economic circumstances. Using Rost s (1991) definition of leadership as an influence relationship among leaders and followers who intend real changes that reflect their shared purposes (102), the mandate of NCLB requires both district and school leaders to enact change among teachers and, by extension, among all students.

As discussed in a variety of texts on educational leadership (Cun ningham and Cordeiro 2003; Guthrie and Schuermann 2010; Kouzes and Posner 2007; Matthews and Crow 2010; Smith and Piele 2006; Whitaker 2010), this requires first that the leader articulates a clear vision that de scribes an achievable reality that is better than the reality that currently exists. This includes a long term goal as well as the short term steps that will make the ultimate goal possible to achieve.

For change to be accomplished, a variety of supporting factors must be addressed in the short term steps that the leader plans, especially given the internal and external complexities of school systems. These factors include the following:

• Articulation of a moral purpose for the change to motivate followers (Fullan 2001a, 2001b; Klimek, Ritzenehin, and Sullivan 2008; Ser giovanni 1992)

 The question that must be repeatedly asked is, How will this *really* help students?
• Training for those who will be required to do new things (Fullan, 1993, 2001a, 2001b; Klimek et al. 2008)

 Change, particularly complex and sustainable change, requires new knowledge and skills, and these are learned over time with structure, practice, and reinforcement.
• Emotional support for followers to take risks safely (Covington 1993; Rogers et al. 1997; Whitaker 2010)

 As with all learning and behavioral change, those who are being asked to try new skills, apply new knowledge, and develop new behav iors require emotional reinforcement and support throughout the learn ing process. They must feel that they can accomplish the desired change and that mistakes are a normal and expected part of the growth process.
• Advocacy for and communication with external constituencies to build support and understanding of the change (Fullan 2001b; Senge 2000)

 Alliances must be built with external agencies and persons who can legitimize the change and assist in communicating the purpose for

the change to others who can potentially impact the school environ
ment.

- Means of assessing the depth and breadth of change as it occurs (Fullan 2005)

    A system for monitoring the acquisition and application of new skills and knowledge and the development of new behaviors must be put into place to determine if anything has indeed changed. This can and should be both informal in personal interactions recognizing changes and for mal through data collection and classroom observations.

- Reflective dialogue with followers to make adjustments as change is enacted (Klimek et al. 2008; Senge 2000)

    Continuous reflection and dialogue among teachers and administra tion is necessary to make sure that change is taking place and that the change process has not itself changed direction through lack of under standing or buy in.

For each of the previously mentioned relational or technical processes to be successfully accomplished, certain organizational structures are required. If these structures are not present in a school system, then the building of these structures as a part of the change process becomes im perative for the leader.

CORE ENHANCEMENT FRAMEWORK

In order to effectively create change in an educational system, research has affirmed the significance of 1) a focus on the technical core task of (a) creating learning environments and (b) aligning curriculum, instruction, and assessment; 2) collaboration among teachers and with administration; 3) continued professional development; and 4) the support of external agencies to provide opportunities for continued growth, reflection, and validation.[2] Each of these elements enhance the core capacity of the school and district, with each element having a direct and reciprocal in teraction with each other element.

The graphic depiction of these change essentials illustrated in figure 1.1 was developed by Baker et al. (2000).

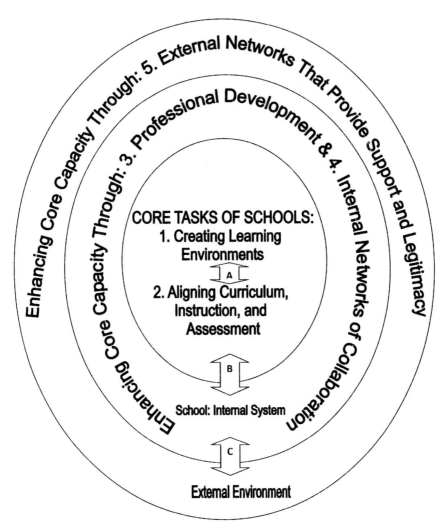

Figure 1.1.   Core-Enhancement Framework of School Development

Source: Reprinted with permission from Baker et al. (2000).

Notes: A = vital connections between core technologies; B and C = vital connections between core technologies and key structures of enhancement. Core tasks of schooling: 1) creating learning environments (e.g., direct instruction, cooperative groups, independent inquiry, facilitating homework, computer assignment, etc.), 2) alignment of curriculum, instruction, and assessment (assuring internal consistency in goals of schooling, means of reaching goals, and assessment to determine attainment of goals).

SUMMARY

Despite the mixed verdict on the impact of the implementation of stan dards on student performance nationwide with math scores up and reading scores relatively unaffected, there is evidence that the adoption and use of standards has positively impacted the performance of minority students (Olson 2006). As state standards have been and are revised to address issues of prescriptiveness or vagueness, several states have demonstrated relatively dramatic increases in student achievement scores.

Several studies have found that strong accountability systems have a positive relationship to the gains these states have made in student per formance on the NAEP, making accountability system consequences the motivation for educators to seriously implement standards based educa tional practices (Olson 2006). Concern regarding the variation among state standards and assessments has led to a recent effort to create national learning standards that could be measured by the NAEP (Cavanagh 2010).

Concerns for educating the whole child to succeed in life and not just on academic examinations, as well as indications that tougher standards and accountability measures may increase student dropout rates (Comer 2006; Kohn 2010; Noddings 2010, Wolk 2006), have not mitigated the mandate for educators to raise student demonstration of learning of cur rent state standards and perhaps future national standards. The demand for reform remains constant, although the processes and products of reform are varied and sometimes elusive.

Arthur Levine, a former president of Teachers College at Columbia University, observes that, we are talking about moving giant bureaucra cies and whole states to improve on the way we get to the standards, in both policy and the classroom (Sawchuck 2010, 19). The premier chal lenge that educators face today is how to respond to this challenge given the variation in resources across schools and districts and the diversity of student backgrounds and needs.

Chapters 3 through 6 describe how district and school leaders build and utilize the core enhancing structures and provide the support necessary to positively change teaching practices in classrooms at each stage in the process of implementing the change of standards based instruction and assessment. As you meet the school and district leaders at various stages in this change process, perhaps you will recognize the steps and structures that you have either led or lived through already as well as gain ideas and insights as to the possible journey ahead.

First, however, you will be introduced to the communities and contexts of the administrators, teachers, and students who shared their thoughts, classrooms, and schools as they navigated the tides of change. Through a description of their communities, you will see that each district and school faced common challenges although each context was different. The demo graphic information given for each district and school address several of the elements taken into consideration by the EPERC in its analysis of fac tors external to the education system that influence students chance for success. It was a combination of these challenges and the unique commu nity context of each leader, as well as his or her educational philosophy, that shaped the perspectives and actions of these eight school districts in the implementation of standards based educational practices.

POINTS TO REMEMBER

- Accountability for student performance has increased dramatically since 1983, when America s public schools were identified as the rea son for the nation s inability to compete in global markets.
- Standards can be impractical to guide classroom instruction if too vague or too detailed.
- Educators generally view standards as helpful guides for curriculum and instruction.
- Consequences for low student performance on state accountability mea sures help to focus educators attention on subgroup achievement but can also restrict the curriculum to only those disciplines tested.
- Social and economic inequities among students are a challenge that all educators must respond to, often with limited resources.
- For schools to improve, a concentration on the core tasks of creating a learning environment and alignment of curriculum, instruction, and as sessments must be supported by professional development and teacher collaboration as well as external networks that provide support and legitimacy.

NOTES

1. The exception being Iowa.

2. These elements have been identified through the work of many educational researchers, beginning with the effective schools movement (Brookover et al. 1982; Crandall, 1982; Crandall et al. 1986; Fullan 1985, 1991; Hargreaves 1984; Huberman and Miles 1984; Joyce 1993; Louis and Miles 1990; Purkey and Smith 1983; Reynolds 1976; Rosenholtz 1991; Rutter et al. 1979; Wilson and Corcoran 1988) and continuing through the current development of professional learning communities and learning organizations (Bryk and Schneider 2002; Darling Hammond 1997; DuFour and Eaker 1998; Glickman 1993; Joyce et al. 1999; National Research Council 2000; Newmann & Associates 1996; Senge 2000; Stigler and Hiebert 1999; Zemmelman, Daniels, and Hyde 1998).

Chapter Two

The Communities and Contexts of Change

Initiatives and mandates play out very differently in individual districts and schools based on how administrators provide motivation and resources to teachers. The actions of administrators vary according to perceived student, school, and community needs. This study was conducted to see how admin istrators have responded to perhaps the largest federal educational initiative and mandate in history standards based education and what changes in actual classroom instruction and student learning have resulted from the ac tions of those administrators.

Districts in diverse parts of a Rocky Mountain state with diverse com munity and student demographics were selected to gain a better under standing of what factors promote and inhibit leadership actions as well as teacher responsiveness to those actions.

The eighth grade was chosen as a focus for several reasons. First, it is often seen as the pivotal year in framing student success in high school. Second, school philosophies and class configurations can vary greatly at the eighth grade level with teachers either working together in a middle school team model or teaching their individual subjects very indepen dently in a traditional junior high school model. Finally, increasing stu dent achievement in later grades is often a great challenge as student mo tivation wanes and social interests sometime seem to overwhelm students on the verge of adulthood.

While the intent of this book is to share what was learned from ad ministrators and teachers regarding their steps in learning and growing into standards based educators and creating standards based schools, the context and challenges of each of the schools in the study are relevant to

understanding how educators respond to both common and unique ob
stacles in school improvement and student achievement. For that reason,
a brief description of the district and school participants is included in this
chapter as well as the data collection methods used.

The names of the districts and schools, as well as individual names, are
pseudonyms to protect the confidentiality of each educator who shared the
hopes, fears, passions, and challenges that guide them as they serve their
students and community.

RESEARCH DESIGN

Superintendents, assistant superintendents, principals, and eighth grade
teachers of language arts, math, and science in eight school districts in
a Rocky Mountain state participated in the study, funded by the Spencer
Foundation. In four large urban districts, two schools were selected from
each district for participation based on student test data, whereas the four
small rural districts each had only one school serving eighth graders, so a
total of twelve schools were included in the study.

The administrators and teachers who participated were interviewed and
also asked to rate their district or school on various aspects of the implemen
tation of standards based instruction and also on their own personal views
of the usefulness of the state s learning standards.[1] At least two classroom
observations of each teacher were conducted as well as observations of
team and faculty meetings. In the larger school districts, a sampling of stu
dents was also interviewed to determine how standards based instructional
practices were perceived by the students. The following is a description of
the communities and selected school factors of each district and school.[2]

DISTRICT AND SCHOOL CONTEXTS

Leader of the Pack

The district that exhibited the most advanced implementation of stan
dards based instruction and assessment practices was the smallest, least
diverse, and wealthiest of the four large urban districts in the study. The

district administrative team of Verde Valley[3] also held the longest tenure as leaders among the four large districts.

The superintendent had served in his capacity for nine years and had appointed the assistant superintendent for instruction and assessment in his second year, elevating her from a middle school principalship within the district where she had worked since 1987 to implement a standards based approach to instructional design. In 2006, she succeeded him as the district s superintendent. The central office team passionately recounted their work over the past decade to implement standards based instruction and assessment practices in the district as well as goals for the future.

Pre dating the state s adoption of content learning standards, the district leadership team initiated the back mapping process to align district curriculum to the proposed standards. The assistant superintendent, Abby McDougall, modeled the K 12 district back mapping process on her successful results at the middle school, noting that, while teachers were ready for more structure from the do whatever you want philosophy of the prior administration, they were not ready for as much structure as the standards required.

With the release of the first year of state assessment scores, however, teachers were ready to do whatever it took to demonstrate and communicate student learning to the public. Although concerned about many aspects of No Child Left Behind (NCLB), Abby noted that the anxiety of consequences related to state assessment performance was a factor that motivated teachers to change and become more open to standards based instruction and assessment.

It became a question not so much of what a teacher or school was doing as what they were not doing for the kids who were not achieving. She made each individual responsible for the students success, Abby explained.

It took eight years for the teachers in the Verde Valley district to really get it, according to Abby. The turning point occurred when the district started sending groups of teachers to national conferences and those teachers would come back and convey the validity of the district s efforts to other teachers in their buildings.

Finding that this strategic investment paid off in terms of teacher buy in, motivation, and openness to new instructional behaviors, the district has continued to send teachers to national conferences in order to build capacity throughout the district. District faculty now frequently present at these conferences and have opened their school doors to teachers and administrators around the country who would like to follow in Verde Valley s footsteps in building a standards based educational environment.

The retiring superintendent observed that it is easy to align curriculum with standards, but it is difficult to actually implement standards based instruction. After aligning the curriculum with the state s standards, the district adopted a district assessment of the standards from the North west Education Association (NWEA) and worked extensively with Mike Schmoker, a nationally known educational author and consultant, to es tablish results teams of teachers at and among grade levels and subjects to analyze assessment data.

While the collaborative analyses of test data built assessment literacy among faculty to a point, the most substantive change in instructional prac tices was triggered by a focus on student achievement demonstrated on classroom assessments. You can align all that, but the idea that every child gets the opportunity to move at their own pace and reassess and all that is more difficult for people to implement, the retiring superintendent explained.

The biggest change for us actually came just in the last couple of years. We changed our whole reporting system, he went on to clarify. And once we did that, then all of the other pieces of the whole standards based came, fell in line after that. So we started actually with a reporting system computerized reporting system that s built on the standards so that teachers can pull standards off and create their own assessments for those standards and then be able to go across the curriculum.

The adoption of a K 12 standards based report card, as well as stan dards based performance assessment requirements for promotion to high school, was the most advanced characteristic of standards based instruc tion and assessment found among all the participating districts and ap peared to mark a philosophical paradigm shift that truly embraced the be lief that all students will be expected to demonstrate essential knowledge and skills. District leaders held meetings with faculty, parents, students, and community members to explain the benefits of the new standards based reporting system and philosophy of student achievement.

Abby cited a student statement in a public forum on the topic as a pow erful explanation of the current assessment system. Many students and parents were upset that their child could take an assessment once and get an A grade, while other students were going to be allowed to retake the assessments and achieve As as well. One student stood up and said, We know you guys are smart, but at least give us a chance to learn what you know, too, Abby related.

The investment of time and resources into educating the faculty and community, providing collaboration time and skills, and developing tech nological assessment and data support was evident in the classrooms of the two schools in Verde Valley that participated in the study. The teach ers and administrators in these schools also spoke appreciatively of the district leadership s repeated articulation of a vision of learning for all students and continuous support of teachers in their own instructional and philosophical growth.

The school with a more diverse and lower socioeconomic status student population received an average but improving rating, even though it did not make Adequate Yearly Progress (AYP) in reading. The more homogeneous and affluent school made AYP in both reading and math and received a rating of high and stable, based on the state as sessment and NCLB subgroup criteria.

The modeling, support, and leadership provided by the superintendent and assistant superintendent were directly acknowledged by both schools administrators and many of the teachers. The provision of resources, knowledge, and continual conversations about student learning were men tioned by almost all the teachers and school leaders interviewed, particu larly in their explanations of how standards have influenced instruction and assessment in their classrooms and the sharing of student performance data among educators and with parents and students.

One teacher observed, A lot of our professional development days are around standards based instruction or assessment. We have a lot of discussions about how to assess and what the function of the report card and the difference between practice and assessment. . . . It s a philosophy change. . . . You have to think holistically.

The role of assessment in guiding instruction, particularly reteaching content and skills, was discussed by each teacher interviewed in the Verde Valley district. Whether it was the development of rubrics, a process that began in earnest more than five years ago according to Abby, or the implementation of the standards based reporting system, the required learning and practice on teachers parts translated to an investment of time as well as energy. One teacher reported spending sixteen hour days each weekend before a report card would be sent out in order to make sure that all the documentation of the students learning was in order to answer student and parent questions.

Once the templates were in place and this teacher gained expertise in identifying levels of proficiency on the standards (a process assisted by her work with colleagues), the work drastically decreased. Although not explicitly stated, this teacher s belief that standards based instruction and assessment was an important goal was conveyed by such statements as I can t help them learn what they don t know unless I have good assess ment data and can go back and reeach what they need to be successful. Verde Valley teachers reported creating more of their classroom assess ments themselves than teachers in any other district in the study, although further assistance in developing sound classroom assessments was on the wish list of one teacher.

The philosophy of all students achieving at a proficient level is evident in classrooms by artifacts and teacher behavior. A teacher made poster in the front of one math classroom boldly announces, This is important! You CAN do this! I won t give up on you! Subject specific learning standards are posted in each room, as in almost all the classrooms visited in this study, but more of the Verde Valley standards were written in kid friendly terms.

The emphasis during classes observed at Verde Valley was more on the criteria and expectation for success in demonstrating learning than on the standards. While critics of standards based education in the cur rent high stakes testing environment warn of teachers teaching to the test or replacing high level thinking skill activities with skill and drill test preparation, this was not evident in the seven Verde Valley classrooms that were observed in this study.

In an English classroom where bilingualism was encouraged among both Latino and Anglo students,[4] students presented PowerPoint analyses of poems with personal reflections on how the selected poem s content was meaningful to the student presenter. Issues of socioeconomic equity and diversity were major themes in the selected works. One student posed the question, Do you think you could be happy if you didn t have all the things you do? while two other students posed questions regarding the struggle of people from different cultures to respect each other and find common ground.

In a math classroom and a social studies classroom, test preparation was the focus of the students activities. Rather than drills, however, stu dents were either working problems or developing essay answers in small groups, sharing their results, and then critiquing their products according to the rubric related to the upcoming assessment.

In Verde Valley, the district administrators assessed the district as being very close to a true standards led model of education. School leaders and teachers viewed the district as in the midst of transition to a standards led educational structure while rating the district as having accomplished var ious aspects of such an educational model. The involvement of students in learning and the articulation of learning goals to students, however, were identified as areas where more growth was needed within the district by teachers and principals as well as district administrators to a lesser degree.

As one teacher explained, I think the student part is still not as clear as it should be. The student part and the family and community part. . . . But the students seem to take more responsibility, and we re clarifying that more and more with the graduation requirements. Here s what you need to know, and they re keeping evidence of meeting standards. Another teacher explained that he asks for student input in developing the rubrics for assess ments after the students look at and evaluate different models or products.

The student input into the assessment process helped students to under stand what criteria needed to be demonstrated and then explained by the student to parents. A language arts teacher observed that our vision is to have the standards go into like a portfolio so when kids complete a task, then that work that they create proves their ability, and they put that in a portfolio, which is a thing in the physical world that you can go through and say this is what I can do. And they can show their parents.

She elaborated on how these portfolios were used, adding, We have these expo nights four nights a year where the parents come in, and they see the work the kids have been doing. In the eighth grade now, since we re doing portfolios, they look through their portfolios, or they look at whatever posters or creations the kids have made, and that to me is what communicates it [learning]. The parent sees what the kid s doing. They see what knowledge they have to have.

The assessment process, as part of the learning process, is viewed as an active and engaging endeavor that encompasses far more than stan dardized test data. Teacher self assessments of the importance of student involvement in the learning process were the highest in Verde Valley of the eight districts studied.

Increased student involvement in the instruction and assessment pro cess, along with greater parent and community understanding of perfor mance criteria, were two immediate goals that teachers and administrators agreed need to work in tandem with the reporting system. When asked what would be a wish for the future to help Verde Valley students learn, the newly appointed superintendent responded, Eliminate grade levels! As discussed in chapter 6, that is perhaps the next milestone marking a truly standards led educational system.

Data Make the Difference

The Eaglecrest School District could be viewed as the second most ad vanced district in demonstrating standards based instruction and assess ment, based on increased student achievement on state assessments. The Eaglecrest district began focusing on standards based education imple mentation out of necessity in 1998 when the first round of state assess ments revealed one of the Eaglecrest schools to be one of the three lowest achieving in the state. This served as a wake up call for district leaders who began investing in teacher training and support systems to increase student mastery of the state s content standards.

The superintendent who shepherded the district through a period of tremendous growth in state assessment scores with the assistance of the director of assessment explained that if a child isn t learning, it s an adult issue. Every adult should feel responsible for every child, describing an attitudinal shift away from I taught it and they didn t learn it. That s not my problem.

Eaglecrest is the largest, least affluent, and second most racially di verse district in the study. Of twenty schools in the state identified by the national Education Trust as being high performing with high percentages of minority and low socioeconomic status students, six of those schools are in the Eaglecrest district (Sanchez Traynor 2006), with one of the schools identified by the Education Trust participating in this study. The

Eaglecrest community has the lowest median family income and cost of living of the participating urban districts. The violent crime index for the community is rated as high.

Participating school student populations reflect greater diversity than the community, with the community reporting 44 percent Latino popu lation and the schools reporting over 50 percent Latino population. At Lakewood school, however, 45.7 percent of the students are eligible for free or reduced lunches, while 72.3 percent of students at Hoover school qualify for free or reduced lunches. Interestingly, despite being the second most diverse district in the study, participating Eaglecrest schools have the second lowest percentage of English language learner students.

While both schools made AYP in both reading and math, Lakewood is rated as a high performing school that is stable, while Hoover is rated as low performing and in decline by the state. Lakewood does have the highest percentage of teachers with at least a master s degree and the highest average number of years of experience.

Although the principal of Lakewood has been there for only three years, he has thirty one years of experience in the district, eleven of those years as assistant principal at a school in the district. The principal of Hoover has five years of experience in her present position and over twelve years of experience in the district at various levels prior to coming to Hoover. District leadership has remained stable for the past eight years, with strong support noted by teachers and principals by the director of as sessment in providing useful data analyses.

While district and school administrators viewed the understanding and use of standards to guide instruction as being standards led, the use of standards based assessments and involvement of students in the learning process were identified as in an initial to midtransitional stage. Teachers in the district reported a higher level of implementation of standards based practices than district level administrators but lower than principals.

In teacher self assessments of knowledge, use, and levels of efficacy in implementing standards based instruction and assessment, Eaglecrest teachers scored themselves the lowest of the four urban districts on fre quency of use of the standards to guide instruction and assess learning, benefits of the standards for instruction and for students, and overall usefulness of the standards for learning. Despite perhaps a perceived need for growth in the implementation of the state s learning standards, schools throughout the district have increased student achievement regardless of demographic challenges.

The director of assessment, appointed and supported by the superin tendent, has worked tirelessly in the past eight years to assemble and distribute data on student achievement throughout the district. The district has provided district and school based professional development opportu nities ranging from how to develop and use rubrics to group development of performance based assessments as well as curricular alignment.

Teachers who had been in the district over three years reported serving on at least one scope and sequence alignment committee. The principal of one school in the study described how she had been a teacher in the district and was   the guinea pig teacher who took her science lesson into a room with seven or eight people and passed out my science lesson and shared it with them. And then they looked at the standards the district had adopted for science and looked to see if indeed the lesson I taught was reflective of those standards.

Many of the newer teachers hired in the Eaglecrest district reported having a firm background in content standards in their undergraduate programs and explained that they relied heavily on the materials either adopted by the district or developed by their peers. Teachers reported utilizing assessments from texts or other district adopted curriculum 60 to 95 percent of the time, with some modification by the teacher of tests and quizzes in the selection or omission of some questions.

When asked their educational philosophy, Eaglecrest educators, both administrators and teachers, frequently included being   standards based in their answers as well as   student centered.   Building a relationship with students in order to better differentiate instruction and motivate students so that   all students can learn   was also mentioned by all but one Eagle crest educator interviewed.[5] While students may be viewed as the focus of the instructional process, teachers viewed the role of students in learn ing as the   recipient,   present and ready to learn, and providing limited feedback to be used to refine instructional techniques.

In the classroom, teachers identified this student role in instruction as reviewing in groups, conferencing with the teacher, and setting achieve ment goals for themselves. Administrators articulated the desire for a much more involved student role where students understand the purpose and outcomes desired in the instructional process and are able to articulate their progress.

In observing classes in the Eaglecrest district, the standards are posted but were directly referred to in both observations of only one math class room in the higher achieving school and integrated into the writing as signment and peer feedback in a language arts class in the more diverse and struggling school in the district that participated in this study. The latter involved students responding to the writing prompt of What would you do if you did poorly on the state assessments? The writing was struc tured as a state assessment situation, and students were instructed to use their writing planners and to include figurative language. Peer critiques followed the writing process.

Throughout the classes observed, an emphasis was placed on the rel evancy of the subject material and skills to career possibilities and com petencies needed in the real world. Two teachers also confessed that they allowed students to retake tests and quizzes or redo work for higher grades, indicating that although that was not the norm, they viewed the demonstration of student learning as the outcome they valued.

The groundwork of curricular alignment appears to have been laid spo radically throughout the late 1990s and then cemented in the early years of the twenty first century. The dissemination of data appeared to be the hallmark of Eaglecrest s standards based education implementation, with district supported opportunities to discuss data among peers and to en gage in standards based professional development.

Communication of learning to students and parents, however, remained traditional, as did the majority of instructional practices. Topping the as sessment director s wish list, however, was professional development on the interpretation of results to improve instruction rather than account ability measures and a user friendly and interactive data warehousing system to retrieve and analyze student information to inform instruction!

Flexible Frameworks and Rubric Awareness

Plainsfield Community School District was the second most affluent community that participated in the study with a median family income of $61,489, a third of its population possessing college degrees, and a cost of living 10 percent above the national average. The community was also predominantly White with a 10 percent Latino population. The schools have the lowest percentage of English language learner students of the four urban districts and two of the rural districts. The district spent the least amount per pupil, $6,834, compared to the other three urban districts and three of the rural districts.

Of the two participating schools in the district, the school with a more diverse population and less stable school leadership, Middlebrook, made AYP in reading and math. The more homogeneous school, Riverview, did not meet AYP in reading but did in math. Both schools were identified as stable in student achievement, although the more homogeneous school, Riverview, was rated high in student achievement, while the more di verse school was rated average.

Middlebrook School had the lowest percentage of teachers possess ing an advanced degree among the urban districts and over a third of the student population eligible for free or reduced lunches. This school more accurately reflected the degree of diversity of the community, while Riv erview reported only 11 percent of its student population to be non White.

The superintendent of Plainsfield came to the district four years ago, bringing thirty three years of educational experience to the job. Both the superintendent and the assistant superintendent were focused on the align ment of curriculum and assessments with state standards and embraced differentiated instruction and the investigation of best practices for spe cific subject content.

As the assistant superintendent explained, We always talk to teachers and administrators that the standards represent the what, but they don t limit the how. So you have a lot of autonomy and we expect you to be creative and innovative and really smart about how you do things. . . . The other thing is you can always supplement the curriculum. It s not all inclu sive and it s not limiting. As such, the standards are regarded as a blueprint for assuring a quality education that encompasses specific skills and knowl edge, and the district s curriculum has been aligned with the standards over the past three years, as have materials adopted by the district.

The district has also offered many professional development classes taught by district personnel to teach faculty how to use the standards to map out their classroom instruction and assessments, focusing on identi fying the assessment before planning instruction. Teachers in the Plains field district reported a greater level of implementation of standards led instruction and assessment practices than did district or school administrators. The teachers also reported the highest frequency of use, perceived benefits, and overall usefulness of the standards in guiding their instruction and assessment practices in the classroom.

With the district providing professional development opportunities within the district and the interpretation of the standards as broad guide lines for instruction, the role of school level leaders to develop the role of standards in the classroom appeared to be greater than in schools with more direct district leadership regarding instruction and assessment devel opment and use. Both schools schedules were structured to allow grade level core subject teachers collaboration time each day, but the outcomes for collaboration were not specified.

The distinguishing attribute of both schools was the use of rubrics to present students with criteria for performance. While the use of rubrics was observed directly in a language arts[6] and a social studies classroom at Riverview and a math classroom at Middlebrook, students repeatedly referred to rubric criteria in asking questions regarding performance ex pectations in science classrooms in both schools as well.

Riverview teachers explicitly recognized the principal s support in standards based instructional and assessment practices, whereas Middle brook teachers appeared to rely on feedback and collaboration among grade level team members alone. This might be attributed to the River view principal having led the school for four years and also serving as an assistant principal at the school for three years prior to assuming the building leadership role, while the principal at Middlebrook was new to the school, having served as a professional development director at the district level prior to assuming the school leadership position.

Teachers at Riverview expressed a desire to have students assume a greater role in the instructional process, including assessment, but ad mitted to some hesitancy in giving up some of the control of learning to students. Classroom observations revealed a high level of trust among teachers and students at Riverview, including high expectations of re sponsibility for completion of work as well as behavior. Interactions between teachers and students at Middlebrook were much more teacher controlled and negative in nature regarding student work performance and behavior.

Cultural Challenges and the Beginning of the Learning Curve

Thorndike School District was the most diverse in school and community demographics of all the participating districts and also the second poor est with the largest percentage of students eligible for free and reduced lunches. The Thorndike community has the lowest percentage of college educated residents as well as the highest rating for violent crimes in the community and unemployment. The Thorndike community was adjacent to a large metropolitan center, sharing several large blue collar industrial areas. The district spent the most per pupil of all the districts in this study and over $2,000 more per student than even the affluent Verde Valley district.

Thorndike had only two middle schools, both of which participated in this study. They were both rated as low in student achievement by the state s department of education. Kesington had been identified as im proving because it met its AYP goals, while the other school, Crestwick, had been rated as declining and did not meet AYP in either reading or math. Principals of both schools are relatively new, in their first and sec ond years as administrators at their schools. The principal of Crestwick, however, had taught for seventeen years in the district (with a majority of that time spent at Crestwick) and was an avid supporter of the work of Richard Stiggins in the involvement of students in the instruction and assessment process. Teachers expressed a great deal of support for princi pals at both schools, particularly at Crestwick, although minimal support for district leadership. School leaders in Thorndike expressed feeling sup ported by district leadership, however.

District leadership in Thorndike has been stable for seven years and appears to be very proactive in community public relations, having initi ated several programs to increase communication with and participation of Latino parents. Large gains had been made on state assessments at el ementary grade levels (a 38 percent gain in reading in third grade scores across the district), and district administrators were intent on duplicating those gains across grade levels. The superintendent of Thorndike was working intently to convey the progress of students to parents and the community at large.

The superintendent of Thorndike came from a business background and brought his focus on the bottom line, in this case student learning, to the district after successful experiences in working with Larry Lazotte in opening an experimental high school in another state and serving as the deputy commissioner of education of another western state at the outset of the standards based education movement. He recruited an anthropologist with a strong quantitative background to serve as the district assessment director, focusing on the development and use of formative assessments that support and guide student learning.

The district assessment director, Jim Connelly, started his efforts with a discussion among district leaders as to what teachers would expect to see as a student demonstration of desired learning outcomes and found the answers to be quite vague. Guided by Marzano s work on establishing clear benchmarks for students achievement, the district initiated the process of backward mapping the curriculum using Reeves s (2003) identification of power standards. This process was completed last year.

Jim observed that their district was probably where Verde Valley was eight years ago and yet that they were trying to reach the same point that Verde Valley was at now but in just two years. Despite high minority and poverty rates and a large number of English language learners, the district leaders expected their students to reach proficiency on the standards despite discouraging research data correlating student population characteristics to test performance.

Although the average years of teaching experience for the two schools were also the average of all schools participating in the study, the teachers participating in the study at Kesington were the most experienced (two of the three in their last year before retirement) and the least experienced at Crestwick (two of the three were in their first three years of teaching).

Thorndike teachers perceived the standards to be useful, but they were uncertain as to the benefits of the standards to them or their students and reported the second lowest frequency of use for planning classroom instruction and assessments.

During classroom observations, the use of standards to plan instruction was the most evident in the science classes at both Kesington and Crestwick. Despite the perceptions expressed on the teacher self assessment instrument, teachers and administrators rated the district firmly in transition to standards based led instruction and assessment in the areas of content standards, adoption, instruction, and student learning. High stakes accountability pressures for immediate test score gains were recognized by district leadership as a factor in limiting efforts to build school and district cultures that encourage teacher learning and growth.

Current district leadership support of school efforts included student led parent teacher conferences in which students shared their NWEA and classroom assessment data. District personnel also conducted workshops with administrators and teachers on how to have conversations about student performance data with colleagues and also with students. Jim s vision for the district was to make data more available via technology that supports teachers ability to help students process information, create, and communicate effectively with others.

Teachers in the Thorndike district were, as district leadership accu rately perceived, at the beginning of the standards based implementation learning curve. Both schools in the district reported the lowest amount of student participation in instruction and assessment, with Kesington teach ers expressing the view that students should not be involved in instruction and assessment. Kesington teachers also reported the lowest perception of benefits of the standards of all eight urban schools. Reflecting those sen timents, little student input aside from answering the teachers questions was observed during classes.

On the Standards Based Classroom Self Inventory, Kesington teachers rated district implementation of standards aligned assessments and stu dent learning the lowest of all participating schools. Kesington teachers also expressed the lowest level of perceived benefits in basing classroom lessons and assessments on the standards of all the schools in the study.

At Crestwick, however, teachers expressed a desire for more student involvement in the instructional process and identified this as both a per sonal and a group goal for the future. More student input into instruction, although teacher guided, was evident in the science and language arts classes at Crestwick. Crestwick teachers also expressed the highest level of perceived benefits in using standards to develop classroom lessons and assessments of all schools in the study.

District and school leaders in the Thorndike district had several cultural challenges that they were confronting. They were attempting to address the cultural challenges of their student population, including language barriers, by providing language classes and bilingual communications to parents to involve them in their children s learning. The teaching culture of the school was in the beginning phases of transition to a standards led educational model with the foundation only recently laid for curricular alignment and the collaborative sharing of student performance data among educators and with students and their parents.

As evidenced by Verde Valley s efforts, the paradigm shift takes time, education, practice, mistakes, and investment of time and effort in the belief that all students can learn and should learn, even if it means changing tradi tional instructional approaches (such as letting students retake assessments). While administrators and teachers alike feel pressured to make changes that increase student achievement in the immediate future, it remains to be seen how quickly such a fundamental change can be made in a manner that is embraced and sustainable as well as how (and if) leaders at the district and school levels can support such a shift in an accelerated time frame.

Fewer Challenges and Less Pressure for Change

The four small, rural districts participating in the study faced fewer di versity challenges in educating the children of their communities and, because of either size or geographic isolation, appeared to have closer informal relationships with parents and the community. This does not mean they were without challenges in demonstrating student performance of state learning standards, but the pressure for change appeared to be less than in urban settings, often leading to delayed efforts to implement standards based educational practices and support systems.

Diversity, Resources, and Achievement

Skyview School District faced many of the same challenges as the larger urban schools, being the largest and most diverse of the four rural dis tricts, with the largest percentage of non White students (36 percent Latino), the greatest number of free lunch eligible students (54 percent in 2005), and the highest percentage of English language learners (25 percent). The Skyview district did not meet AYP goals in either reading or math but was still identified by the state as average and stable in student performance.

Broadmoor Community School District, located adjacent to an urban setting, had a less diverse student population (21 percent Latino with

8 percent English language learners) but was expecting an increase in minority students in the coming decade. Broadmoor also spent the least amount per pupil of districts studied, although the cost of living and me dian family income was only slightly below the state average. The district did not meet its AYP goals in either reading or math but was rated as average and stable in student performance.

Tumbleweed and Farmington school districts were the most geographi cally isolated of the four rural districts with very small minority student populations (3 and 5 percent, respectively). These two districts also spent the most per pupil of all the participating districts in the study, with Farm ington spending the most at $12,149 per pupil. Students living in poverty or English language learner populations could not be reported by the Tumbleweed district in the past two years because of the small number of students who fell into these categories.

Both districts met AYP goals in reading and math, having twelve and six performance targets, respectively, compared to the thirty plus targets identified for the other ten schools in the study. Tumbleweed was rated as average and stable, while Farmington was given an average but in decline rating. In each of these farming communities, the violent crime index was lower than the state average and lower than any of the urban districts in the study. With the exception of Broadmoor, the administra tion and teaching staff were very stable with most educators choosing to work in the community because of family ties that frequently extended over several generations.

Leadership Stability and Perceptions of Standards-Based Education Implementation

The district and school leadership in Tumbleweed was the most stable of the four small districts with a very flexible and collegial atmosphere among district, high school, and elementary school administrators. Ad ministrator perceptions of the district s implementation of standards based instruction and assessment fell into the moderate stages of transition to a standards led educational system. Teachers perceived lower levels of implementation, particularly in the area of classroom assessments and student learning. Self assessment of teacher use, efficacy, and benefits of state learning standards were lower than in the large urban schools but very consistent among the rural schools.

In the Tumbleweed district, school level administrators collaborated with teachers on the analysis of student data and provided some opportu nities for teachers to attend professional development outside the district. Participation in state assessment scoring workshops was reported by teachers to have greatly increased their understanding of what students need to do to demonstrate proficiency of content standards and adjusted their instruction accordingly. Many of the teachers in the Tumbleweed district have participated in curriculum alignment and development com mittees in the past three to four years as well.

Of the four rural districts, the use of technology to communicate stu dent progress among faculty and parents was most strongly embraced in Tumbleweed, with one teacher developing a database to correlate state and district (NWEA) assessment data with classroom assessment data. Rubrics that teachers developed were evident in student assessment preparation as well as in feedback to students on their demonstration of knowledge and skills relating to the learning standards. Particularly in the language arts classroom observed, peer critiques using the state writing rubric and teacher student conferencing played large roles in student instruction.

School leaders structured the daily schedule to allow for grade level team meetings, and teachers acknowledged support from administrators to grow professionally to increase student learning. The teachers attributed the support of school and district leaders to a desire to increase students life opportunities rather than because of state accountability pressures.

In the Skyview district, new district leadership in the past two years brought a renewed focus on standards based education implementation. District administrators sent teachers throughout the district for training at Richard Stiggins s Assessment Institute, implemented NWEA district testing, and initiated more discussion of student performance data among teachers. Although the district engaged in back mapping of the curricu lum in alignment with the standards when they were newly adopted in 1998, the focus on alignment of classroom instruction and assessments was not maintained and can be recalled only by teachers who have been with the district for seven or more years.

In recent years, curricular alignment with standards appeared to have become more of an endeavor of individual teachers than a coherent district process among collaborating teachers. The new administration s focus on assessment data appeared to be increasing collegial discussions among

and between grade level teachers as well as the sharing of data with stu
dents. At Skyview Middle School, teachers held conferences with each
student to discuss state and district assessment data and to set individual
goals for increased proficiency of the standards. Classroom, grade level,
and school rewards were given for student attainment of those goals. In
creasing numbers of English language learners and students eligible for
free or reduced lunches have spurred district and school level adminis
trators efforts to more effectively educate these subgroups of students to
avoid state accountability consequences.

Broadmoor Community School District s superintendent was new to
the district, having been in the job only three months when he was inter
viewed. He explained that the district is currently engaged in mapping the
curriculum and is also building up their database of student performance
assessment information. The district has moved away from using the Terra
Nova as a district assessment and was in the process of adopting Scantron.

Broadmoor s superintendent was also pushing for an online acces
sible grade reporting system for parents to access and wanted more time
for teachers to collaboratively examine student performance data. In the
implementation of standards based education, the superintendent saw the
standards as clarifying what is to be taught and assessed. Using a teacher
in his former district as the role model, he explained that, ideally, students
should be able to understand the standards and know where their weak
nesses are and what they need to do to increase their performance.

Teachers in the Broadmoor district viewed the district as close to be
ing standards led but still in the later phases of transition, which is much
higher than the principal s or the superintendent s evaluation of the dis
trict s progress. Guidance of instruction by the standards was the area that
teachers felt was the strongest in their district, with student involvement
or knowledge of standards based practices being the weakest area.

The average increase in state assessment scores for eighth graders in
reading, writing, and math was the highest of any school in the study. The
middle school principal had a great deal of expertise in addressing student
learning needs, having a master s degree in special education and serv
ing as a special education director in another district, and has completed
all the course work for her doctorate in curriculum and instruction. She
viewed the district as being a little slow in aligning the curriculum with
the standards, sharing the perspective that many small districts waited to

begin their implementation until several years after the standards were ad opted by the state. The daily schedule is structured to provide a common planning time for each grade level core subject team.

The middle school principal was a strong supporter of standards based education and has endeavored to stimulate the sharing and analysis of student performance data among grade level teams. Working closely with the prior district leader, the principal had assisted her faculty in identify ing learning targets based on the standards and moving from a text based curriculum to a process of professional selection of best practices and ap propriate materials to address the learning targets using data.

She has also hired a retired teacher, described as a curriculum leader, to assist teachers in completing their mapping and reevaluation of the cur rent curriculum. So far, however, the mapping is still in a skeletal stage. The data mining that the principal has worked on with her staff includes the data available from the state education department and the Alpine data system.

The implementation of six week grading periods throughout the year and the online grade reporting system placed teachers in a position of providing students more opportunities to start over and achieve and a greater aware ness by teachers of timely feedback on assignments and tests. Although the principal expressed the belief that her teachers were being guided in most of their instruction by the standards, she saw it as her responsibility to keep the process of learning going and implementing or refining instructional practices as well as using data to guide instruction. If I stopped here, she shared, most of what we would do would sit on the shelf.

The practice of giving tests prior to instruction to determine the stu dents learning needs is another innovation that the principal had imple mented, explaining to teachers that this isn t a mystery game! They need to know what they are expected to know and do. The use of learning options and rubrics were two of the changes that she reported seeing in her school as a result of standards based instruction implementation.

Of the school s eighth grade team, two of the three teachers were new to the district, and one was new to the profession, having completed an alternative certification program. Each teacher reported that the standards guided his or her instruction. In each of the classrooms observed, student interaction in groups and whole group sharing predominated with stu dents appearing highly engaged.

The math classroom most explicitly demonstrated standards based in struction. In each lesson observed, the teacher had students work on prob lems or a project in small groups and then shared their efforts. In working problems on the board, the teacher frequently stopped to ask the class how they should present this to ensure the full points possible according to the state s assessment rubric.

Farmington School District was the most atypical of the districts partici pating in the study. The community had one paved road that ran through the town from east to west and another that intersects the highway and runs to the north. There was one restaurant in town, one grocery store, and one gas station. The district and school administrators reported that school athletic events are frequently attended by most of the community s members.

None of the teachers at the junior/senior high school possessed a mas ter s degree, and the average class size was eight, the lowest of all par ticipating schools. The cost of living was the lowest of all communities in the study, and the median family income was the lowest of the four rural districts although $2,000 higher than in the Eaglecrest urban district. District leadership was stable, although the school leader was just starting his second year in the district and in a leadership position.

The superintendent explained that getting student performance infor mation out to parents had been his priority the past two years. He hired a data coordinator who helped to create a road map of each student s prog ress using math scores and state assessment scores to convey to teachers the strengths and weaknesses of each student. The principal also used the data to assess the impact that teachers have on groups of students. Teachers agreed that they have had many meaningful conversations with the principal about standards, especially for the state tests, and we have had staff meetings talking about the state test results and what is expected from us as a staff to help ensure our AYP.

Teachers in the Farmington school reported that they planned their in struction and assessments based on the state standards and were mindful of student performance on state assessments. Instructionally, the influence of standards in the classroom was directly observable and articulated to students.

In the science class, assessments and instruction are explicitly tied to the content standards, and students worked on answering questions in class according to the state assessment rubric requirements. Having taught in California, the science teacher in Farmington explained that he often referred to the California benchmarks to gain a clearer understanding of what specific knowledge and skills his students needed to demonstrate to meet proficiency requirements on the state assessment.

Although diversity and language barriers were not challenges in the district, the teachers explained that the isolation of the community often led students to a very limited view of their life options and decreased perceptions of the importance of academic attainment, making student motivation a very real challenge. Relationships between teachers and stu dents families appeared to play a significant role in encouraging student performance in the classroom. A high incidence of drug use by students and parents, particularly meth, also was reported by teachers as an im pediment to student learning.

Instruction and assessment methods were very traditional although slightly less so in the science classroom, where more student collabora tion was encouraged. Although greater student involvement was desired, the language arts teacher viewed that as a future goal. As a requirement for her alternative certification program, her lessons were tightly tied to the state s content standards, and the standards were posted although not always articulated to students.

The role of students in the instructional process prompted the district leader to recall one of his favorite teachers and began to identify student involvement as a key to that teacher s impact on his learning as well as elements of instruction that teachers in the district utilized that were very effective in engaging students in the learning process. Interestingly, the school leader stated that students did not have a role in the instructional process. The disparity among administrator and teacher responses high lighted a lack of dialogue, let alone consensus, on this topic.

POINTS TO REMEMBER

The stories told by the administrators and teachers in each district, along with the instruction observed in the classrooms of each school and teacher interactions, painted a picture of how learning standards were viewed and how those views were translated into pedagogy on a daily basis both in and out of the classroom. Some of the lessons to be learned from their experiences include the following:

- Diversity of student population increases the challenges that educators face to meet state accountability requirements.
- Funding resources vary greatly among school districts regardless of student population subgroups identified as low performing.
- Administrator perceptions of the benefits and level of implementation of standards based educational practices are more positive and accurate than teacher perceptions.
- Linkage of lessons and assessments to state learning standards do not result in pedagogical changes.
- District and school leadership is necessary for teacher learning and growth that results in instructional changes that support student learning (see tables 2.1 and 2.2).

NOTES

1. Of the two instruments used, the *Standards Aligned Classroom Initiative* survey was developed by MetriTech (2001) and the *Colorado Standards Based Classroom Self Inventory* was developed by the SBE Design Team (1996).

2. Community demographic information was obtained from the U.S. Census Bureau in 2007, and school demographic and performance information was ob tained from the state s department of education in 2007.

3. All district, school, and personnel names used are pseudonyms.

4. After asking a boy to close the door in Spanish, the teacher smiled at him and said, You are going to get an A in Spanish next year and be fluent by the time you go to college!

5. That educator focused on his use of modeling instruction and student practice.

6. During one observation in the Riverview language arts class, the teacher asked what she always talks about for them to get a good grade, and a student answered, The standards! The answer the teacher was looking for was for them to refer to their rubrics.

Table 2.1. Participating District Community Demographics

	Large Urban Districts								Small Rural Districts				
School	Pearsall	Gallup	Middlebrook	Riverview	Kesington	Crestwick	Lakewood	Hoover	Tumbleweed	Broadmoor	Farmington	Skyview	State
District	Verde Valley		Plainsfield		Thorndike		Eaglecrest						
District population	16,176	16,176	71,093	71,093	20,991	20,991	102,121	102,121	982	5,117	534	2,690	
Median age	36.2	36.2	34	34	29.8	29.8	36.5	36.5	44.3	35.4	36.3	38.2	34.3
Community White, %	83.8	83.8	76.8	76.8	42.5	42.5	51.1	51.1	95.3	61.4	96.6	85.4	69.1
Community Latino, %	13.3	13.3	19.1	19.1	52.9	52.9	44.1	44.1	2	37.2	3	12.6	12.5
Unemployment rate	4	4	2.5	2.5	4.3	4.3	4	4	4	5	4	5	5
Median family income	57,373	73,697	61,489	61,489	39,792	39,792	32,985	32,985	38,906	39,094	35,000	55,144	55,375
Cost of living, % of U.S. average	119	161	110	110	95	95	82	82	81	81	79	98	98
Community BA+	33.1	33.1	31.3	31.3	3.7	3.7	16.8	16.8	15.2	14.5	7.9	21.8	32.7
% White, 18 or younger	30	30	36.9	36.9	38.9	38.9	29.8	29.8	29.4	35.1	33.5	36.7	32.8
Violent crime index*	2	5	4	4	6	6	6	6	2	2	1	1	3
Community population	5,533	2,907	81,238	81,238	27,651	27,651	103,625	103,625	996	5,227	569	3,348	

* 1 = low; 6 = high.

Table 2.2. Participating School Demographic and Academic Performance Information

	Pearsall	Gallup	Middlebrook	Riverview	Kesington	Crestwick	Lakewood	Hoover	Tumbleweed	Broadmoor	Farmington	Skyview	State
School White, %	36	62	78	64	18	27	45	38	96	61	95	79	64
School Latino, %	62	37	19	33	76	67	50	57	3	36	5	21	26
Free lunch eligible, 2004	25	14	10	22	75	62	29	59	37	NA	NA	NA	
Free lunch eligible, 2005	44.5	21.3	14.5	31.3	86.1	75.3	45.7	72.3	NA	54	30.3	24	32
English-language learners, % 2005	53	36	11	19	43	40	17	18	NA	25	8	8	14
Teachers with MA+, %	49	49	46	33	42	52	65	50	65	34	0	33	49
Average years of teaching experience	5	8	10	11	11	11	13	9	14	11	10	16	11
Student-to-teacher ratio	14	16	21	18	18	17	18	16	16	14	8	17	18
Principal, years	11	1	4	1	2	1	2	4	4	4	2	5	
Prior principal, years		2		7		1							
District revenue per pupil	8,067	8,067	6,834	6,834	10,126	10,126	7,606	7,606	10,219	7,280	12,149	6,585	
Rating*	2	3	3	2	1	1	4	1	2	2	2	2	
Academic improvement**	3	2	2	2	3	1	2	1	2	2	1	2	
AYP target, 2005	30	30	36	36	38	36	36	36	12	32	6	32	
AYP targets met, 2005	29	30	33	36	38	32	33	34	12	30	6	30	
Met AYP reading***	1	2	1	2	2	1	2	2	2	1	2	1	
Met AYP math***	2	2	2	2	2	1	2	2	2	1	2	1	

* 0 = unsatisfactory, 1 = low, 2 = average, 3 = high, 4 = excellent.

** 1 = decline, 2 = stable, 3 = improvement.

*** 1 = no, 2 = yes.

Chapter Three

Stage 1: Initial Alignment—
The Beginning of the Journey

OVERVIEW OF LEADERSHIP AND TEACHER ACTIONS

Initial Alignment Stage (two to three years' average duration)

Leadership actions that occur in this stage are the following:

- The district leader publicly identifying a need for standards-based edu cational practices.
- The district leader then enlists and empowers other district-level and school level leaders to work with faculty on developing standards based instructional practices.
- A curriculum coordinator is identified to assist with the alignment of grade level content to state learning standards.
- Texts and other materials aligned with the state's standards are adopted.
- Workshops and in-service presentations on rudimentary standards-based alignment concepts, goals, and practices are scheduled by the district.
- In-service or monthly collaborative time is allocated to align the cur riculum with the state s learning standards.

Teacher actions that occur in this stage are the following:

- Back-mapping of the curriculum to align with the learning standards begins.
- Teachers attend informational sessions intended to create buy-in and also to build knowledge and skills.

- Teachers begin examining and comparing their grade-level content and matching it to the state s learning standards. This is aided by the adoption of prealigned texts and materials.
- Teachers identify coverage of standards in lesson plans.
- Toward the end of this stage, teachers produce outlines of content in each subject and for each grade level that is aligned with the state s learning standards, reducing content overlap and eliminating lessons that do not overtly advance the students learning of the standards.

DISTRICT PRIORITY IDENTIFICATION

The implementation of standards based education in a district begins with the articulation of a need for standards to guide instruction in every classroom by the district leader, the superintendent. In the district that made the most progress in implementing standards based instructional practices, Verde Valley, the superintendent enlisted the leadership of a progressive principal who had bought in very early to the use of standards to guide classroom instruction and promoted her to the position of assistant superintendent. As a team, the two district leaders held a series of meetings with parents in each of the communities served by the district to explain the need for educational standards and how that would impact students learning.

These district leaders also enlisted the help of the Parent Teacher Organization, beginning with the elementary schools and working their way, over time, through the middle and high schools. These meetings were held during the first year of staff development provided to teachers in the elementary schools. The leaders of Verde Valley invested in sending groups of teachers to national conferences to reinforce the need for the instructional change to use standards to guide classroom instruction. They care about kids and it was trying to get them to look at their practices that might be more effective, the assistant superintendent explained.

While Verde Valley s leadership carried their vision and message directly to parents as well as teachers from the start, most district leaders demonstrated their commitment to implementing standards based educational practices by creating district level leadership positions that were charged with carrying out staff development related to the standards. This included the creation of director or assistant superintendent positions for curriculum. These district level positions were then given the resources to present informational sessions and workshops or in service activities to faculty.

The first step taken by these new leaders was to enlist the faculty s efforts to align the curriculum to the standards. Breaking down the standards into language that teachers understood or a definition of what each standard looked like in student learning was the initial challenge, as many standards were very broad or vague. Districts frequently used resources and training from professional development providers such as Larry Ainsworth, Douglas Reeves, or Heidi Jacobs to identify the power standards or to unwrap the standards and make them usable in a class room context for teachers.

The districts that brought in outside experts or consultants to initiate and/or guide this process progressed through this initial alignment phase more quickly than districts that attempted to guide the process through the use of school and district personnel alone. Although many districts first approached alignment of what was currently being taught at each grade level to the standards, the need for congruence throughout and across grades pushed them to undertake a back mapping of the entire district s curriculum in the core subjects.

This process of backward design was most clearly and popularly ex plained and promoted by Wiggins and McTighe (1998) in *Understanding by Design*. Their book became the guide in districtwide curriculum align ment for many districts. The first subjects aligned, of course, were the disciplines to be tested first by the state s assessments.

Following the back mapping process, districts invested in textbooks and other curriculum materials that correlated and supported the state learning standards and the newly revised local curriculum. Training then was provided throughout each district on the use of these new materials and texts, usually by the manufacturers of these materials. The actual use of materials, however, was up to each teacher. The person responsible for monitoring what happens in a classroom, the building principal, was the essential key to ensuring that this new initiative of standards and curricu lum alignment was implemented in classrooms.

Although district leaders focused on faculty training, they first met and had long discussions with school leaders who would be leading the alignment process at the school level. At this stage, the principals role was to facilitate the process of matching the pieces together, putting the standards together with what is taught.

The adoption of new texts and materials also required that the principal also oversees that the new curriculum is being used in classrooms. The buy in and support of the building leaders were essential for the accom plishment of the alignment of the curriculum and the consequent use of the curriculum to guide what actually transpired in each classroom on a daily basis.

THE ROLE OF THE PRINCIPAL IN TEACHER LEARNING

The tricky part of the change process is getting people to become open to different behaviors than what they are accustomed to doing. Before you can change behavior, you have to change the thoughts on which those behaviors are based. Such changes are usually triggered by a disorienting dilemma that create[s] an opportunity for reflection and redirection, or may occur when an accumulation of internal dilemmas create a growing sense of disillusionment (Glickman, Gordon, and Ross Gordon 2009, 45). Novice teachers experience many disorienting dilemmas in the first few years of teaching as they learn to bridge the theory that they have learned in their teaching preparation programs with the reality of helping students to learn.

As such, new teachers are often hungry and searching for guidance, even if they are hesitant to seek it out and risk the perception of inad equacy. Experienced teachers, however, are often wedded to their favorite classroom units and projects and become indignant and balk when asked to give up the bird nest building project that they do with their fourth graders that has become a school tradition just because it doesn t relate to any fourth grade standards.

The principal is the pivotal person in helping teachers resolve this dis sonance in a productive manner as much as sometimes creating the situa tion that created the dissonance. As such, the principal plays an essential role in teacher learning and the implementation of change.

While a district must invest the initial material resources to provide time for teachers to accomplish the work of aligning their curriculum with state learning standards and the training on how to do that effectively, it is the principal who must provide the support for the endeavor, repetitively stating and demonstrating the importance of the effort and validating the outcome of those efforts. The principal must also show support and in crease his or her understanding of the curriculum to be implemented by attending the curriculum alignment sessions with teachers.

It also falls on the principal as the supervisor and evaluator of teach ers to provide accountability for demonstrating the use of the new cur riculum in the classroom. This must be left up to not the required one or two classroom observations but, rather, more frequent observations and dialogues with teachers. The walk through method of quick observations and feedback has become widespread as a method of monitoring more closely what occurs in a classroom on a regular basis.

Statements made by teachers in this stage address the alignment of the curriculum with the state learning standards and the adoption of new cur ricular materials but do not indicate any change in instructional method. In response to the question of the impact of the state s standards on in struction, teachers in the alignment stage answered with the following:

- "We adopted a new curriculum this year. We picked the series . . . be cause of the standards.
- "I am fortunate because our textbooks were written with the standards."
- "I have gone through every single standard and tried to touch base on just about everything sometime during the year.
- "It gives me a guideline and keeps me focused."
- "The standards themselves have kind of focused what it is I need to teach. I m still not in a place yet where I am looking at the standards for everything I do in my classroom. We just finished writing a writing curriculum this summer. There was a committee of us and the standards helped guide [us as to] here s what we re going to teach.

TEACHER COLLABORATION

Research has shown that learning is a social process and that new knowl edge and behaviors are most successfully reinforced when embedded in daily work. Perhaps the most important aspect of teacher learning in this initial alignment stage is the collaborative time that is given to teachers to share ideas and frustrations and to construct a common basis of practice. This collaboration time breaks down the traditional isolation of teachers.

Nearly fifteen years ago, the National Commission on Teaching and America s Future (1996) called for the isolation of a teacher in a classroom behind a closed door to be replaced with a free and frequent exchange of meaningful information regarding student performance among educators so that the core processes of schooling could be effectively developed to increase student learning. In many schools, collaboration among teachers to align standards and curriculum is a first in working together toward a professional goal that many teachers experienced.

This initial collaboration among teachers, with the support of school leaders, sets the stage for the further engagement of teachers in the work necessary to change instructional practices. Exploration and adoption of new instructional strategies, as well as how instructional decisions are made, are hallmarks of the second stage in the process of implementing standards based educational practices, which focuses on the alignment of instruction with learning standards. Teacher teams or professional learn ing communities developed in the second stage and advocated over the past two decades by researchers and practitioners alike are predicated on this initial collaborative alignment effort (Holcomb 2009).

CORE ENHANCEMENT ELEMENTS IN
THE INITIAL ALIGNMENT STAGE

In the initial alignment stage, district and school leaders focus efforts on one element of the core technology or tasks of schooling, that is, the align ment of curriculum and instruction with state learning standards. In order to accomplish this task of alignment, leaders must allocate the resource of time (by paying substitutes to cover classes or providing stipends for work outside of contracted hours) for teachers to collaborate.

First, teachers collaborate to identify what they have taught at each grade level and come to a common understanding of what each standard means in terms of student learning. Collaboration then focuses on the correlation of content to state standards and the identification and elimina tion of redundancies in the curriculum as well as adopting and using new materials to support the newly aligned curriculum.

Districts must also provide professional development for teachers to understand the standards, align the curriculum, and use new curricular materials either through district personnel or the support of outside agen cies or consultants. The external provision of support in professional development accomplishes the goals of this stage more effectively and expediently, supporting progress toward the second stage of standards based education implementation.

During this stage, at least these three elements of the core enhancement framework are required to lay the groundwork for standards based educa tion implementation and provide internal school structures that support further teacher growth and collaboration in the use of student data to guide instructional practices to support student learning of learning standards. These elements are identified in the context of core enhancement elements in figure 3.1 as elements 2, 3, and 4.

MOTIVATIONS AND CHALLENGES

Each of the districts studied was motivated to adopt the state s learning standards as the basis of the curriculum by student performance on the state s assessment of student learning of the standards. In all but the two smallest rural districts, an increase in minority student populations high lighted the lack of success the schools were experiencing in educating all students. The performance of students from lower socioeconomic status backgrounds also provided motivation for every district, as the lack of performance of students eligible for free and reduced lunches was brought to the attention of each community as well as state officials.

The four larger, urban districts that were forced to confront these chal lenges with larger percentages of their student populations and responded more quickly and invested more resources than the smaller, rural districts that felt less pressure because of smaller underachieving student groups. Farmington and Skyview school districts, serving communities of fewer than a thousand citizens, did not have enough minority students to be required to disaggregate data for the state assessment, and 30 percent

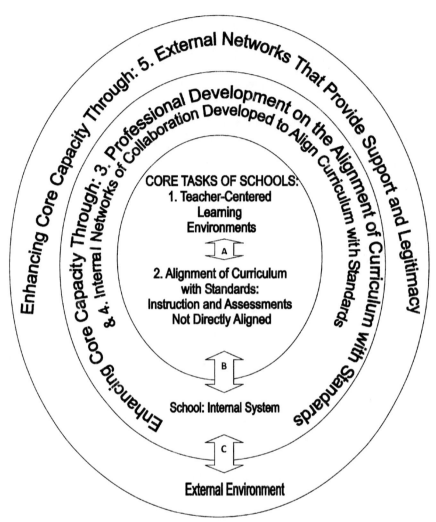

Figure 3.1.   Core-Enhancement Framework Elements in the Initial Alignment Stage

or less of their students were eligible for free or reduced lunches. Both schools serving eighth graders in these districts met their Adequate Yearly Progress (AYP) performance targets, the number of which was a third to a sixth less than the AYP targets of the larger schools.

While the state s accountability system served as a common denominator in the motivation of district leaders to embrace standards based education, the lack of underachieving student populations did not provide any motiva tion for Farmington and Skyview schools to move through the stage of initial alignment and on to the second stage of using data to inform instructional practice. Interestingly, district and school administrator perceptions of the implementation of standards based education fell into the moderate range, indicating a perceived transition to a standards led educational system.

Teacher perception of the implementation of the standards to guide ed ucation was lower than that of the administrators, particularly in the area of classroom assessments and the impact on student learning. Teachers self assessment of their use, their efficacy, and the benefits of the state learning standards were also lower in Farmington and Tumbleweed than in the other large urban districts and two other rural districts.

Although a few teachers in Tumbleweed had taken it on themselves to learn more about collecting and communicating data on student per formance of the standards, these efforts were individual and isolated. While teachers in these districts conducted practice sessions for the state assessment, district and school leaders did not invest additional resources to increase teacher learning and use of classroom data to change daily instructional practices.

For the districts and schools that moved through the initial alignment stage, the duration of the alignment process took between two and four years, depending on the resources invested by administrators. Verde Valley completed the alignment process in only two years but, drawing on a com paratively wealthy community tax base, was able to invest more resources than the other districts in providing teacher training, both by the district and by outside professional consultants, and collaboration time. Districts with fewer financial resources moved through the alignment process more slowly but within three years of beginning their efforts, with the exceptions of Farmington and Tumbleweed, which did not progress beyond this stage.

POINTS TO REMEMBER: MOVING ON TO STAGE 2

To advance to the second stage of standards based education implementa tion, the following must occur in stage 1:

- Identification of a curriculum leader at the district level
- Alignment of local curriculum with state standards
- Alignment of curricular materials with state standards

- Utilization of aligned curriculum and materials in classrooms
- Establishment of a structure for collaboration among teachers
- Support for ongoing teacher collaboration by administration
- Professional development to support alignment and use of aligned curriculum, including an understanding of what student learning is associated with specific standards

REFLECTIVE QUESTIONS FOR PRACTITIONERS

Reflective Questions for District Leaders

1. What do you think standards based instruction looks like in the classroom? (What do you want to see teachers and students doing?)
2. Who have you communicated your vision of standards based instruction to and with what degree of detail? What rationale did you provide for the implementation of standards based instruction?
3. What professional development resources have you allocated to align the curriculum with the state s learning standards? What training has been provided to building leaders and teachers to align classroom instruction with the standards?
4. What evaluation system has been put into place to monitor the alignment and use of a standards based curriculum in classrooms?

Reflective Questions for Building Leaders

1. What do you think standards based instruction looks like in the classroom? (What do you want to see teachers and students doing?) How does this align with your district s vision of standards based instruction?
2. How have you communicated your vision and support of standards based instruction to teachers and parents? What rationale did you provide to enlist teacher support in the implementation process?
3. How has the curriculum been aligned to the state s learning standards? How has this changed classroom instruction?
4. What resources do you need to support your teachers in aligning the curriculum and their instruction with the state s learning standards? How can you obtain these resources?

5. How do you support and monitor teacher collaboration in aligning the curriculum and instruction with the state s learning standards?

Reflective Questions for Teacher Leaders

1. What does standards based instruction mean to you, and what does that look like in a classroom? How does it impact student learning?
2. What is the vision of standards based instruction held by your district and building leadership?
3. How is your instruction guided by the state s learning standards?
4. How do you know students in your classroom are making progress on the standards?
5. What additional knowledge and skills or other resources do you need to fully align your instruction to support your students learning of the standards? How can you obtain these?
6. How do you collaborate with other teachers to ensure that all students are learning the same knowledge and skills required by the standards?

PORTRAIT OF A TEACHER IN AN EARLY INITIAL ALIGNMENT STAGE SCHOOL

Textbook Alignment and Traditional Teaching

Peggy Schofield is a first year high school English teacher in the Farmington School District.[1] Peggy doesn t like to lecture, explaining that she learns the best from reading and writing, so she has her students work on grammar and writing exercises in small groups frequently. The district adopted textbooks that are aligned with the state s standards, so Peggy feels that by covering the texts, she is covering the standards. She spends a great deal of time creating her lessons plan and referencing which standard she is covering for every class activity, something her principal has stressed as important.

Peggy says that the standards have not changed how she approaches what she does in the classroom at all, relying on the test supplied by the textbook to assess student knowledge. Peggy would like to eventually feel comfortable enough in her knowledge of student assessments to assess students using formats other than tests and quizzes and use rubrics to as sess their knowledge.

She has had several classes in her teacher preparation program on as sessment and looks forward to attending workshops in the future to find out how to actually use authentic assessments and rubrics in her class room. Her immediate goal is to review the state assessment sample ques tions so that she can go over those with her students.

During class, Peggy leads her students through sample grammar exer cises written on the board and then has them work individually on exer cises in the text. On writing days, the students go to the computer lab, and she monitors their progress, correcting their grammar, punctuation, and structure when they turn in their drafts. Just as the building she teaches in, Peggy s method of teaching English is traditional and dependent on students working through the text in reading, grammar, and writing.

PORTRAIT OF A TEACHER IN A LATE INITIAL ALIGNMENT STAGE SCHOOL

Ready to Move On

Julie Biggs has taught for thirteen years, spending ten of those years in the Tumbleweed School District. She started her professional life as an elementary teacher but made the move to teaching middle school lan guage arts six years ago after briefly teaching Title I computer classes in the district.

Her goal as a teacher is to inspire her students to learn and be a part of their learning, giving them all the opportunities they need and to push themselves. Julie believes that her students need to know where they are at and where they are going as readers and writers. When they re in class, that they re actively participating in it and not just sitting there and hoping it ll sink in, you know the things that you are throwing at them. . . . It doesn t work for all the kids, you know, but we re working on it.

Julie s biggest frustration is assessment. There are tests but not assess ments that she can use to guide her instruction. She feels that the standards have helped to focus her teaching but that they don t guide everything she does in the classroom. Over the past summer, she served on a writing cur riculum team that used the standards as a guide, and she felt good that she was already covering many elements included in the standards.

There is a poster listing the language arts standards on the wall, but Julie notes that the students don t notice it. I don t necessarily visit with the kids as much as I should about, Here s the standard we re working on and this is what our goal is to achieve. Still, it s one of a hundred million things we have to accomplish.

Julie remembers attending a local workshop on using graphic organiz ers to align what was going on in the classroom with the state s learning standards, but it was filtered out because it was just too cumbersome. We went through changing our administration, and the workload it entailed was just too much. She also attended a state assessment scoring confer ence that she enjoyed. The district has also just started using a district assessment, but she isn t sure yet how useful that will be to guiding her instruction.

Julie uses spelling and vocabulary building materials and the district s reading series as resources but prefers to create a majority of the tests and activities that she uses in her classroom. She does this on her own because she is the only language arts teacher at her level in the district. Her district has just started using an online grade reporting system that parents can access to see grades and missing assignments, but letters sent home and parent teacher conferences are the main means of communicating student learning to parents.

If she could have more time and computers, Julie feels that she could better individualize learning for her students. Five computers sit in a corner of her room, but she explains that only two are currently working. During her classes, she tries to hold individual writing conferences with each student at least twice a week.

Students in her classes complete reading contracts and let Julie know when their revisions are complete so that she can meet with them, mark ing technical errors and suggesting improvements. Julie teaches grammar by working through a paragraph written on the board with the whole class, reviewing the appropriate rules, and then letting the students work together on worksheets.

Julie has students grade one another s writing as well, using a rubric based on the state s writing rubric. She also spends time having the stu dents work through test ready booklets and reviews test taking strate gies and the importance of doing well on the state test with them on a regular basis.

NOTE

1. Each of the teacher portraits included in chapters 3 through 6 highlight an eighth grade language arts teacher in order to underscore what is done differently in each stage in the same content area.

Chapter Four

Stage 2: Transitional Data— Digging Deeper with Data

OVERVIEW OF LEADERSHIP AND TEACHER ACTIONS

Transitional Data Stage (three years' average duration; four to seven years into the standards implementation process)

Leadership actions that occur in this stage include the following:

- An assessment coordinator is identified at the district level to work with school leaders and teachers.
- A district assessment system is implemented that complements state assessments but also provides more frequent, timely, and/or detailed feedback on student performance on the state s standards.
- Building-level leaders schedule collaborative time for teachers to exam ine the data from district and state assessments.
- Standards-based professional development is provided for teachers through the district leadership with assistance from an external expert.
- Teams are typically formed and professional development focuses on team effectiveness, data analysis, the development of rubrics, and the classroom development of effective student assessments of learning.
- Assessment workshops that develop teachers' skills in developing ru brics and scoring student work typically are scheduled by district lead ers at this stage.
- Toward the end of this stage, the district develops a database correlating available student performance assessment data with district and state as sessments as well as an online grade reporting system that is accessible by parents as well as teachers.

Teacher actions that occur in this stage include the following:

- Teachers begin to identify essential learning ("power standards," benchmarks, and so on) based on their own perceptions of what is re quired for students to perform successfully on state assessments of the learning standards.
- There is generally less reliance on texts or externally prepared aligned materials as this stage advances.
- Teams of teachers analyze data and, toward the end of this stage, begin developing common classroom assessments and share student perfor mance data on these assessments.
- Teams become more cohesive and adopt a perspective of shared respon sibility for student learning.
- Toward the end of this stage, teachers may begin identifying criteria for student demonstrations of proficiency on standards and/or benchmarks.
- Classroom assessment rubrics also begin to be developed by teams of teachers, and performance data are shared on a limited basis with stu dents.
- Teachers begin creating and sharing classroom assessments based on the standards with peers.

DISTRICT AND SCHOOL USE OF DATA

The second stage of standards based education implementation begins with a new emphasis on collecting and using student achievement data at the district level. Resources are invested in the creation of a district level assessment coordinator or the identification of an assistant superintendent who is responsible for overseeing the coordinated administration of as sessments across the district at the school level and the analysis of the assessment data collected.

The first charge given to these new district assessment leaders by their superintendents was to adopt a districtwide instrument to assist with more closely monitoring student achievement on state learning goals at each grade level in order to provide teachers with more specific data to guide classroom instructional decisions. The data gained through these district assessments were to provide teachers with multiple data points of student achievement to chart student progress on state learning standards, en abling teachers to identify what skills and knowledge students lacked and to adapt classroom instruction accordingly.

Four of the six districts that progressed to this stage adopted the North west Evaluation Association s (NWEA) Measures of Academic Progress (MAP) assessment to monitor student progress on learning goals. The MAP test is administered through a computer program that begins by ask ing students grade level questions for each learning goal and then adjusts the difficulty of the subsequent questions based on students performance. This format is used to provide a challenging test for every student, according to NWEA (http://www.nwea.org/sites/www.nwea.org/files/resources/MAP%20Basics_Overview_0.pdf).

Student performance is reported in terms of a Rausch Unit (RIT) that is then linked to a continuum of skills and concepts for reading, language usage, mathematics, and science that are aligned to each state s learning standards. Teachers can compare a student s RIT score to where that stu dent s score falls on the learning continuum and identify what skills and concepts that student may be ready to learn and structure their classroom instruction for each child accordingly.

The reading, language usage, and math test can be administered up to four times each year, providing four data points in an academic year to monitor and adjust student instruction, as compared to the single annual data point provided by most state assessments. (The science test is recom mended to be administered three times each academic year.) NWEA also provides growth norms for each grade level so that teachers can see how close to grade level progress is being achieved by each student throughout the year.

One district in the study first adopted a districtwide grade level assess ment from TerraNova but was contemplating changing to a Scantron as sessment based on the perception that more detailed student performance data to guide classroom instruction would be provided by the Scantron instrument. The TerraNova assessments were developed and have been available through McGraw Hill since the late 1990s. Used heavily in California, the TerraNova assessments were updated to reflect 2007 state standards. Both Scantron and TerraNova provide online assessment for mats and a variety of formats and materials to assess students both annu ally and throughout the year.

All the assessments selected by the districts studied provided profes sional development for teachers and classroom instruction support materi als that assist teachers in linking assessment data to classroom content in struction. The available support packages range from online or site based teacher workshops and conferences, data banks of grade and skill level questions to use for weekly student progress assessment, to classroom instructional materials to teach every section of each learning standard.

Given the availability of professional development materials and sup ports from these assessment suppliers, the district assessment coordinator must decide how district resources can be used to most effectively mine the data provided by the selected assessment. The amount of materials that districts can purchase is dependent on the financial resources avail able to them.

PROFESSIONAL DEVELOPMENT
AND TEACHER COLLABORATION

Early in the transitional data stage, district assessment leaders provided resources for groups of teachers to attend professional development work shops, particularly through conferences or on site workshops. Districts typically selected one teacher from each grade level or, in larger districts, two or three teachers at each grade level in schools across the district. These teachers were frequently expected to share what they had learned with grade level peers in their schools using a training of trainers model to build teacher assessment capacity throughout the district.

The team structures developed in the initial alignment stage for the back mapping of the curriculum and the identification of essential learn ing targets were used to disseminate the knowledge gained by professional development attendees to fellow teachers. The format used to report the data from these district assessments required teachers in several of the districts studied to further refine the district s essential learning targets to align with the adopted assessments.

Even as districts progressed through the transitional data stage, this investment in professional development regarding assessments continued. Verde Valley annually sent at least thirty teachers and administrators to national training sessions to ensure that educators new to the district had a solid knowledge of the district s assessment practices and philosophy.

As one teacher in the district explained, We spent a lot of time our selves learning about what standards based really means. It s a philoso phy change. It s a totally different way of thinking about education, and so you really have to figure, instead of asking yourself, Is this a good student?, you ask yourself, Can they do this one thing?

Team Data Analysis

Building level leaders initially provided in service time for teachers to meet and analyze the new district assessment data but soon found it necessary to provide more frequent collaboration time for teachers to discuss the new assessment data in terms of classroom instructional decisions. The incorpo ration of common planning time for teacher teams occurred in the middle of the transitional data stage. Teachers reported enjoying looking at student data together in teams. It is very hands on interaction rather than any sit and get or anything like that, one Thorndike teacher observed. Additional professional development was provided by several districts on team data analysis, such as Schmoker s (2001) results on team development.

The principal was responsible for making sure that each grade level team was analyzing the assessment data deeply and really using the data to guide their instructional practices. Team discussions would identify which skill or knowledge section of the assessment rubrics students were performing low on. Teachers would then plan their instruction to reteach and reassess those areas.

Principals attended team meetings on a rotating schedule, communicat ing to each group the expectation that they must understand the data in terms of what classroom student achievement looked like in order to pro vide the appropriate instruction to bring students to that targeted level of learning. What does the student data show you? was a frequently asked question, both by principals and among teachers. Principals also asked teachers to justify their instruction based on their knowledge of student performance data.

Teachers were asked to answer such questions as How much time are we spending on teaching each concept? and How are we teaching it?

Building level leaders were held accountable by district assessment coor dinators for the answers to such questions. This provided opportunities for teachers to begin to reflect upon what doesn t work [and ask] What did I do? This reflection on instructional practice is essential for teachers to begin to question, experiment, and change their pedagogy or become what Sch n (1984) described as a reflective practitioner.

As Senge (2000) emphasizes in his articulation of schools as learning organizations, reflection is critical for behavior changes. While an indi vidual might select one set of data to add personal meaning to in order to make assumptions, draw conclusions, form beliefs, and base actions on, interactive reflection adds multiple perspectives of what the data are and influences the assumptions formed, conclusions drawn, beliefs developed, and actions that result from the reflective process.

Peer interactions also encourage reconsideration of personal views and reconnection to alternative perspectives and approaches and allow for reframing of thoughts and actions. As brain research has repeatedly supported, learning is social, and the institutionalization of collaborative structures that allow teachers to reflect together over student achievement must be established for pedagogical growth. Engaging in reflective dia logue is also considered a core element of successful professional learning communities (Matthews and Crow 2010).

Professional Learning Community Development

Although only one of the schools studied referred to their teams as profes sional learning communities (PLCs), the structural elements described as essential in several PLC models developed by Hord (1997), DuFour and Eaker (1998), and Blankstein (2004) were developed in schools in the transitional data stage. Effective collaboration in PLC models includes the following, according to Matthews and Crow (2010):

1. A shared sense of purpose
2. Participation in collaborative activities
3. A focus on student learning
4. Deprivatization of teaching practices
5. Engagement in reflective dialogue

The teams developed in the transitional data stage are formed for the shared purpose of aligning classroom instruction with state learning stan dards and examining student data gathered from district assessments. To be meaningful, classroom practices are then linked to the student perfor mance data as teachers examine what they are doing or not doing that is leading to the student performance that is being demonstrated.

Matthews, Williams, and Stewart (2007) identified ten cultural elements of successful PLCs that are also characteristics of schools in transitional data stage schools. These include the leadership actions that support Matthews et al. s cultural elements (Matthews and Crow 2010) (see table 4.1).

Whether the teams are called PLCs or the schools set out to establish learning communities, the structures that are required for schools to use stu dent data effectively are the same. This perhaps accounts for the increasing

Table 4.1.   Correlation of Leadership Behaviors in the Transitional Data Stage and Matthews, Williams, and Stewart's (2007) Ten Cultural Elements of Successful PLCs

PLC Cultural Elements	Transitional Data Stage Leadership Behaviors
1. Common mission, visions, values, and goals that are focused on teaching and learning 2. Focus on student learning 3. Participative leadership that focuses on teaching and learning	Principal leadership that participates in team meetings to set and maintain a focus on student achievement through assessment data analysis
4. Decision making based on data and research 5. High trust embedded in school culture 6. Teaming that is collaborative	Principal leadership that supports and encourages teachers in changing curriculum and instruction to meet student needs (risk taking)
7. Interdependent culture that sustains continuous improvement in teaching and learning 8. Use of continuous assessment to improve learning	Development of teacher teams to examine student performance data in order to align classroom curriculum and instruction with state learning standards to increase student achievement through ongoing reflective dialogue
9. Professional development that is teacher driven and embedded in daily work 10. Academic success for all students with systems of prevention and intervention	Reflection on classroom instructional methods by teachers and changes to instructional methods as indicated by student performance data, with investment of additional professional development resources by district and building leaders as requested by teacher teams

adoption of PLC models as a means of school reform to increase student achievement. In the schools studied, these structures are established midway through the transitional data stage. Building leaders and teachers who reach this point, however, realize that more can and must be done to impact student learning.

Development of Common Classroom Assessments and Rubrics

At the midpoint in the transitional data stage, teachers began creating common assignments as classroom assessments based on the standards in response to district assessment data to gather even more data to moni tor student progress. District and building level leaders responded to teacher and principal requests for assistance in this process by providing additional professional development, either through district personnel or external assessment providers, on protocols for examining classroom assessments and the development of rubrics to identify norms of student performance on those classroom assessments.

The benefits of this systematic analysis of student performance are well elaborated by Ainsworth and Viegut (2006). The development of rubrics for common classroom assessments enables teachers to compare student performance across individual classes.

Principals again play a significant role in moving teacher teams along to this point in their implementation of standards based education. A principal in the Thorndike district who had spent several years provid ing training for various districts on establishing essential learning targets based on the state s learning standards led the development of common assessments with teaching and coteaching units that used integrated com mon assessments.

The development of common grade level classroom assessments and corresponding rubrics to gather data on student performance from these assessments is a significant step in the transitional data stage. Teachers early in this stage still rely heavily, if not solely, on textbook, district, and state assessments for data to determine student learning progress. There was a wide range of teacher responses from schools at all levels of the transitional data stage in identifying what percentage of classroom assess ments they created as compared to assessments they used directly from textbook manufacturers or other external assessment providers.

While a few teachers said that they created approximately 25 percent of their classroom assessments, the majority of teachers in this stage felt that they created, either individually or through work with their teams, 50 to 60 percent of classroom assessments. Six teachers in schools in this stage or who had moved into the third implementation stage reported creating 90 to 100 percent of their classroom assessments.

The creation of common classroom assessments and the means for meaningful sharing and analysis of student classroom performance, how ever, marks a shift in teachers views of the locus of responsibility for collecting data, indicating also a new valuing of student performance data and the use of the data. The difference for one teacher in the Plainsfield district is an emphasis on the application rather than the theoretical use of data. Assessments developed at this stage are formative rather than sum mative. This also changes how teachers communicate instructional goals to students.

COMMUNICATION OF EXPECTATIONS TO STUDENTS

As teachers work together to develop common assessments and use the student performance data gathered from those assessments to monitor and assess student progress toward learning standards, they begin to see value in using the data to involve students in the learning process. This happens in varying degrees, depending on how far into the transitional data stage the school leaders and teams have progressed.

Initially, this will include the requirement by building leaders that instruction and assessments are explicitly linked to student data and per formance standards in lesson plans. Subsequently, it is represented by the posting of standards and achievement targets in classrooms and teacher references to these standards and targets throughout classroom instruction.

A Thorndike teacher explained that he has been trying to make sure that the kids know what we re working on by having it really big on the wall and then, This is the standard that we are addressing, and pointing to it on a regular basis so that they see the connection of where we re going and what we re doing. At this point, communication of learning targets to students is relatively superficial but is used by teachers as a justification for classroom work to students. The standards are no longer viewed as pertinent only to teachers but as potentially pertinent to students.

In the rural district of Skyview, principals were asked to work with their grade level teacher teams to use both state assessment and NWEA assessment data to have students set performance goals for each district and state testing period. In explaining the role of students in the instruc tional process, a math teacher at Skyview Middle School explained that students take classroom tests and receive feedback on how they had done, and the teachers realized that the students also needed to receive feedback on the district and state assessments in order to feel accountable for their performance.

The Skyview math teacher explained that the students really didn t have any results or there wasn t really anything that they could be held accountable for, so starting this year, we have taken their NWEA scores and their state assessment scores, and we ve talked to them about them. We tell them where they re at, where they should be at the end of the year, and then the students write goals about how they are going to get to that point. This teacher added that the students really did like it and that, when they identified where they were at, they were more motivated to reach their learning target for that year.

The principal of Skyview Middle School kept track of student progress for each class and planned a reward for the class that had the most stu dents reaching their learning targets by the final district assessment.

Beyond just sharing assessment data with students to set learning goals, schools further into the transitional data stage also shared performance on classroom assessments to communicate to the students how they were progressing in demonstrating their learning for each standard.

The principal of Crestwick School in the Thorndike district explained that we re in the process of helping teachers shift the responsibility for achievement to kids by actually making them partners in exploring their own data and measuring their own work against a set standard, which is usually the rubric. Our goal is that kids will take the ownership. I keep saying to our teachers, You take responsibility for instruction; let them take responsibility for learning. So we do that by making them partners in their own self evaluation.

Rubrics allow students to have a clear understanding of what consti tutes successful or proficient demonstration of their learning. In order to clearly articulate what the demonstration of learning looks like, teachers at this stage expose students to models of student work that represent different levels of proficiency in demonstrating learning of a standard and ask students to identify how particular elements of the standard are represented. This in turn gives the students an even clearer idea of what the learning target looks like, potentially making that target more acces sible to them.

References to guide teachers in the creation of rubrics and effective feedback include Arter and McTighe s (1998) *Scoring Rubrics in the Classroom: Using Performance Criteria for Assessing and Improving Stu dent Performance*, Tileston s (2004) *What Every Teacher Should Know about Student Assessment*, and Brookhart s (2008) *How to Give Effective Feedback to Your Students*. Several districts used the work of Richard Stiggins (2007) to guide teachers efforts to articulate performance targets to students, with one district sending teams of teachers to conferences and workshops held by Stiggins s Assessment Training Institute.

Student Involvement in Assessment and Learning

In the later transitional data stage, teachers begin sharing even more responsibility for learning with students and involve them in the develop ment of rubrics based on the models teachers share with students. Guides such as Ainsworth and Christinson s (1998) *Student Generated Rubrics: An Assessment Model to Help All Students Succeed* are used in this pro cess.

Students benefit from this process in the following ways:

- *Student Motivation:* People naturally want to know how well they have performed on a given task. Students who evaluate their own work and the work of others using the assessment criteria that they helped create are more motivated to perform well.
- *Understanding Assessment Criteria:* By asking students to apply the assessment criteria they helped write, a standard for acceptable perfor mance is established. Students internalize this standard and understand what the resulting grade means.

• *Reinforcement of Content:* During the assessment process, students are reviewing content related to the unit focus questions. Students are searching their performance task projects to verify that they have the content required by the rubric, which continually reinforces their own understanding of the material presented (Ainsworth and Christinson 1998).

The involvement of students in the identification of performance cri teria in the demonstration of learning of standards and monitoring of progress also indicates a significant shift in the perspectives of teachers from the process of learning as teacher centered to more student centered, as advocated by Wiggins and McTighe (1998), Tomlinson and McTighe (2006), Stiggins (2007), and many other educational assessment authori ties. This shift is difficult for many, if not most, teachers.

In response to the question of what the students role should be in the learning process, most teachers in the transitional data stage agreed that students need to know what their learning goals were and know what they had to do to reach those goals based on their current performance. They need to know this is where I am, this is where I m heading, and then here s how I m going to get there, so by conferencing with them, visiting with them, being up front with them, they have that buy in and they take part of it themselves, one teacher explained.

Linking student involvement in learning to the assessment process, a teacher in the Verde Valley district shared his belief that students should know not just the criteria of the assignments but also what skills they are trying to build. A teacher in the Broadmoor district described it as show ing students what they need to do to move ahead and move forward, use that as a road map and then have the lessons become student led where the kids can say, okay, this is differentiated instruction. This is what I m working on today because this is where I m at and this is where I need to go.

Teachers in this stage also emphasized that student selection of or input of assessment methods was a form of student involvement in the learning process. One teacher mused that, the kids just go ape when I tell them they don t have to take a test if they d rather act out a skit!, seeing her students motivation as directly related to their role in selecting how they are assessed on their learning.

The assistant superintendent in the Eaglecrest district felt that the role of students in instruction and assessment should be expanded. Students should be involved in the analysis and dissemination of results to their peers and community. Additionally, students should be able to provide feedback on the nature of the assessment, as well as their preparation for the assessment. Both administrators and teachers used the word should frequently in describing the role of students in the learning process.

Many teachers expressed support for greater student involvement in the learning process, from identifying criteria for the demonstration of learning to alternative methods of demonstrating their learning, but most felt that they were not yet to that point in their classrooms. One teacher explained that she was not yet ready to give up that much con trol of the learning process to her students, although she understood the potential benefits such involvement could lead to in student motivation and learning.

A teacher in the same district attributed her lack of student involvement in the learning process to the state s accountability system: They are the recipients. They don t have much say in the matter, literally. You know, there s just so much material that has to be covered, and they have to be responsible for it, and so they re just sort of on the receiving end of, you know, the judgments that we re trying to make in their best interests.

Although issues of giving up teacher centered control of learning and external accountability pressures characterized most teacher responses in schools that were well into the transitional data stage, there were also a few teachers in schools early in the transitional data stage who believed that showing up prepared for class (with the definition of preparation ranging from having a pencil and having eaten a good breakfast to having studied for the test or completed the homework) was the extent of the role that students should play in their own learning. The teachers who identi fied these very limited roles of students had received limited professional development.

Communication of Learning to Parents

The final indicator of standards based education implementation in the transitional data stage is communication of student achievement of state learning standards to parents. This first takes the form of the development or adoption of an online grade reporting system that ties student classroom performance to learning standard targets. The next step in communication with parents is a sharing of detailed information of how students perform on the district and state assessments of the learning standards.

Administrators and teachers recognize that accessibility to this student information is limited by parental access to and familiarity with technol ogy and that this limitation is greater for parents of low socioeconomic status students, many of which are also English language learner (ELL) students, who generally perform lower on district and state assessments than their more affluent peers whose sole language from birth is English.

Traditional reports of student progress, such as progress reports sent home with students at various weekly intervals, school report cards mailed to parents, and parent teacher conferences or beginning of the year open house events, were viewed as the alternative methods of com municating with parents who did not have technological access to the online data systems.

Many teachers also discussed the use of notes sent home when students did not turn in homework or were failing a class as well as teacher notes in student assignment books. With the exception of parent teacher con ferences and e mails from parents, the communication regarding student learning was predominantly one way, from teachers to parents, with lim ited opportunities for dialogue between parents and teachers.

CORE ENHANCEMENT ELEMENTS IN THE TRANSITIONAL DATA STAGE

In the transitional data stage, alignment of assessment and instruction with curriculum and the state s learning standards occur under the leadership and supervision of a district assessment coordinator. The creation of a learning environment with some student involvement in the learning pro cess begins to occur later in this stage although unevenly among teachers throughout schools in a district. These changes within the context of the Core Enhancement Framework are depicted in figure 4.1.

Internal networks of collaboration are strengthened as teacher teams are provided additional time and guided by building leaders in analyz ing student assessment data, first examining district and state assessment

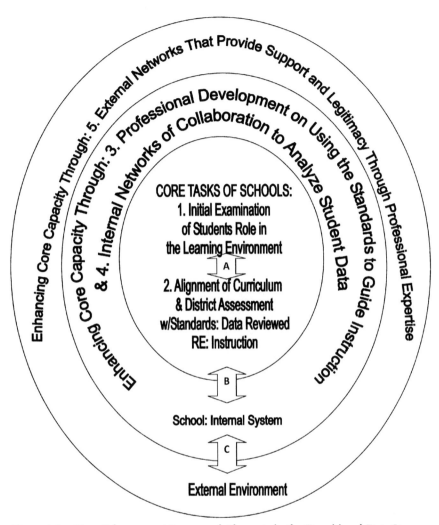

Figure 4.1. Core-Enhancement Framework Elements in the Transitional Data Stage

data and then developing common formative classroom assessments and rubrics to analyze classroom data on a regular basis. Professional develop ment is initially provided by districts at the beginning of this stage to help teachers make sense of newly adopted district assessment data to identify where each student is at in achievement of the learning standards and what skills and knowledge the students lack.

External networks that are engaged in this stage include providers of professional development regarding assessment materials, systems, and

related instructional decision making. Additional professional develop
ment is also often provided as teacher teams request additional support in
developing classroom assessments and rubrics.

The means of professional development varies according to district re
sources, with the most affluent districts sending groups of teachers from
every grade level and building administrators to national conferences
and trainings and less affluent districts purchasing books or hiring an in
service day speaker and using district level personnel to facilitate teacher
learning of data analysis and use as well as assessment techniques.

MOTIVATIONS AND CHALLENGES

The districts and schools that moved into the transitional data stage had
adopted textbooks and instructional materials aligned with the state s
learning standards but found that this did not impact the achievement of
most students, particularly the performance of students from low socio
economic status backgrounds and ELL students, both group that were
increasing in number in these districts. The districts that advanced through
this stage were those that had significant if not majority populations of
poor and ELL students.

The schools that moved the most quickly through this stage were led by
superintendents or district assessment coordinators and principals who very
clearly and repeatedly spoke of the importance of student achievement of
the standards to teachers. These districts and schools also invested more
professional development resources and provided collaboration time to
teachers to make sense of whatever student assessment data were available
and searched for ways to strengthen the monitoring of student progress.

The urgency to address low student performance by at risk subgroups
on the state assessment was a primary motivator for the educational lead
ers at the district level to invest resources to support the implementation
of standards based instruction in schools, even when those resources were
limited by local economic conditions. Limited resources were a challenge
to the smaller and poorer districts in this stage, but many stretched their
professional development dollars by using the training of trainer model
and providing professional development opportunities using district per
sonnel.

Building the knowledge base of all educators, building leaders and teachers, regarding how to evaluate and use student data to guide class room instruction was the biggest challenge encountered by each district in the transitional data stage. Hargreaves and Fullan (1998) coined the phrase assessment literacy to explain this vital skill that teachers must possess to effectively use student performance data.

Assessment literacy includes the following:

1. The capacity to examine student performance data and results, and to make critical sense of it
2. The capacity to act on this understanding by developing classroom and school improvement plans in order to make the kinds of changes needed to increase performance (Fullan 2001b)

The term data has often been associated only with standardized test scores, which are frequently of little use to teachers to make classroom instructional decisions (English 2000; Popham 2003, 2010; Stiggins 2007; Wiggins 1998). The understanding and interpretation of stanines and quartiles is something that few teachers have undertaken willingly or seen as relevant to their teaching. With the adoption of No Child Left Behind, standardized testing of state learning standards made the test results more important to educators but no more useful.

Wiggins, Stiggins, and others, such as the National Research Council (2000, 2001), have presented persuasive arguments as to why teachers must develop the knowledge and skills necessary to gather information or data on student performance in each classroom that can be used to guide instructional decision making.

In this second stage of the implementation of standards based educa tion, educators must embrace and explore the potential for classroom data to promote student learning. This is a significant change in how teachers define and use assessments and the resulting data collected that requires the acquisition of new knowledge and skills as well as behaviors in and out of the classroom.

In addition to developing an understanding of types and uses of assess ments, reliability and validity issues, and how to analyze and use data from a variety of sources, teachers in this stage are also asked to change their professional behavior toward each other and collaborate. The very private and independent instructional decision making process described by Lortie (1975) becomes open to examination and input from others. This can be a scary process if the norms of trust and mutual support are not part of the school s culture or quickly established among team mem bers. It falls on educational leaders to support the establishment of col laborative structures and relationships in this stage.

Another challenge that is encountered later in the transitional data stage is the issue of what role the student should play in the instructional pro cess, including assessment. While Wiggins and Stiggins urge for a change in pedagogy that explicitly includes assessment that is student centered, this is an additional hurdle for teachers who feel that they must dictate the instructional process if their students are to reach the learning targets as sociated with the state s standards. After all, the significant consequences of student performance on the state assessment of the standards impact teachers rather than the students.

The changes asked of educators, particularly teachers, in the first stage of the implementation of standards based education are small compared to the changes required in the transitional data stage. Beliefs regarding data and professional interactions must change, and all the barriers associ ated with change must be addressed by those leading this change. Resis tance to change can take many forms, from active opposition to passive nonparticipation, and be justified by a variety of rationales.

O Toole (1995) compiled a list of thirty three rationales against change, including the following: homeostasis, stare decisis, inertia, satisfaction, lack of ripeness, fear, self interest, lack of confidence, future shock, futility, lack of knowledge, human nature, cynicism, group mediocrity, ego, short term thinking, myopia, ideology, fallacy of exception, and habit. To navigate and mitigate the vast range of barriers that people and groups erect in response to pressure to change, a plethora of books have been written.

A perhaps simplistic summary of how educational leaders can support the individual and organization changes that surface in the implementa tion of standards based education include the following:

- The establishment of trust between leaders and followers throughout the district and in each school
- A clear statement of the goal of the change and what the benefits of ac complishing this goal will be

- The provision of the means be it knowledge, skills, materials, or time to accomplish the goal
- A safe environment where mistakes are accepted, perhaps even ex pected, as part of the learning process
- Shared responsibility for the outcome of the change

For people to be willing to step out of their comfort zone and risk fail ure, they must have an idea of where they are going and why, trust that the direction is correct or at least necessary to explore, have the means to get there, and feel that their involvement is necessary for the journey to be successful. This is, in essence, what promotes student learning as well as adult learning, and learning is a process of change.

The districts and schools in the transitional data stage learned and pro gressed at different rates, depending on the amount of pressure generated by low student achievement and pending consequences from the state s ac countability system. The average duration of the stage was three years across the six districts that had moved into this stage, however. Two of the districts that were in their fourth and fifth years of the effort to implement standards based educational practices were in the early part of this second stage.

Another district that had been working on the implementation for six years was midway through the transitional data stage, and a fourth district that had been addressing standards based instruction for seven years was in the latter part of this stage. The familiarity of the district assessment coordinator and building leaders with the use of data and assessment methods appeared to influence how quickly collaborative structures were created and how teacher teams began to use and search for more and bet ter data on student performance.

At this stage, as in the initial alignment stage, knowledgeable and articulate leadership assisted teacher growth and changes in classroom practice. Only one district studied advanced into the third transitional as sessment stage.

POINTS TO REMEMBER: MOVING ON TO STAGE 3

To advance to the third stage of standards based education implementa tion, the following must occur in stage 2:

- Adoption and use of a district means of assessing student progress on the state s learning standards at frequent intervals throughout the school year.
- Teachers have a clear, common understanding of student performance targets for each grade level.
- Teachers, led by their principals, meet on a regular basis to discuss student performance data.
- Professional development is provided to teachers and building leaders on how to collect, analyze, and use student performance data to guide instructional decisions in the classroom. This includes the development of common classroom assessments and the development of rubrics to identify clear criteria of performance expectations.
- Development of a district database of student performance that is acces sible to parents as well as teachers.

REFLECTIVE QUESTIONS FOR PRACTITIONERS

Reflective Questions for District Leaders

1. How is student progress on the state s learning standards monitored in your district? What additional information would better inform teach ers to guide student learning of the standards?
2. How is student performance data collected and used in your district? How is this data used to guide classroom instruction?
3. How do teachers collaborate in your district? What purpose has been communicated regarding teacher collaboration? How is teacher col laboration supported and nurtured? What role has been communicated to building leaders as to their role in teacher collaboration?
4. How are building leaders held responsible for teacher use of student performance data?
5. What additional knowledge or skills do building leaders and teachers need to effectively use student performance data to guide classroom instruction?

Reflective Questions for Building Leaders

1. How do teachers monitor student progress on the state s learning stan dards in the classroom? Does the information that teachers collect on

student progress guide classroom instructional decisions? What infor
mation would assist teachers in making classroom instructional deci
sions pertaining to student progress in learning the state s standards?

2. How have classroom instruction and assessments been aligned to the
   state s learning standards?
3. How have teachers identified key performance targets for students?
4. What is the purpose of collaboration among teachers in your building?
   How have you articulated this purpose?
5. How assessment literate are your teachers? How can you help more of
   your teachers to become assessment literate?

Reflective Questions for Teacher Leaders

1. What student data do you collect and use to inform your instruction?
2. How do you determine the criteria for student performance in your
   classroom?
3. How do you use rubrics in your classroom? Why do you use rubrics?
4. How do you determine what type of assessments to use in your class
   room?
5. How are your assessments aligned to the state s learning standards?
   What information do your assessments provide to you regarding stu
   dent progress on the learning standards?
6. How do you share student performance data with colleagues? Why?
7. How have the standards changed how you teach and assess students?
8. What do you see as the role of students in the learning process? How
   can you more actively engage students in the learning process?

PORTRAIT OF A TEACHER IN A LATE
TRANSITIONAL DATA STAGE SCHOOL

Meredith Sizer has taught language arts for four years in the Plainsfield
School District, all at Middlebrook Middle School. Prior to coming to
Middlebrook, she had taught adult living classes in the community and
also worked as a school psychologist. Meredith feels that learning needs
to be meaningful to students and relevant in terms of today s world and
its challenges. She tries to keep her lessons high in interest and energy

for the students. She says that the standards are her focus in teaching and that everything she does in the classroom is standards based, drawing on the knowledge and skills she has gained in course work offered through the district.

She relies on the input and feedback from her Professional Study Team to develop assessments and rubrics. Meredith explains that the team is made up of teachers from all the subjects taught at the eighth grade and that they try to take an interdisciplinary approach in teaching the stan dards, often sharing student work samples and results from classroom assessments, because the knowledge and skills covered by the state s learning standards are not discrete but apply to multiple disciplines.

Although the district s textbook series is correlated to the state s stan dards, Meredith reports that her team makes up almost all of their own assessments, although they do borrow ideas from the textbook s assess ments sometimes. She sees her team moving toward having more student input into the development of rubrics and assessment methods but notes that students already have multiple options as to how they will demon strate their learning in many areas. She struggles with what she character izes as giving up control of her classroom and the learning process but says she knows that it is important for students to own their learning and that it will increase their learning.

Meredith, like her peers, has several students in each of her classes that are ELL and some that require a bilingual teacher in the room to assist those students with understanding directions. Posted on her whiteboard at the front of the room are the standards and specific skill and knowledge targets that the students will be working on that day.

Meredith goes over the sequence of what the class will be working on and refers to the standards to explain why they are doing this particular activity. Assignments, tests, and quizzes are referred to as assessments, and Meredith reviews those grading criteria and the reasons for the vari ous points on the criteria before each assessment.

One day, before a final draft of a mystery story was due, Meredith handed out an editing guide with a rubric for the paper to the students, along with red pens. She went over each criteria item (point of change, dynamic character change, point of view, creation of suspense, sentence tags, word choice, title, paragraphing, and grammar), stopping for stu dents to critique and mark items on a peer s draft after each explanation.

Even though it was a large class of twenty seven students, each student was quiet and on task throughout the period. Meredith reminded them, Some of you are looking at proficient and some of you are looking at advanced [on the rubric] because that is what you want your final product to be.

Although no bell rang, Meredith announced that it was break time, and the students quietly and courteously tended to bathroom breaks or trips to the drinking fountain or lockers or ran errands to the office or other classrooms. At the end of the ten minute break, the students were all back and ready to get back to work on adding to their graphic organizers on a detective story that they were reading and using as a model for their own writing.

As students again worked in pairs or trios, they busily compared ideas and good quotes that they found that they thought they could use to make their own writing more effective. There was an air of mutual professional ism among the students and teacher that was refreshing but rare.

Chapter Five

Stage 3: Transitional Assessment— Redefining the Learning Process

TRANSITIONAL ASSESSMENT STAGE (THREE TO FIVE YEARS' AVERAGE DURATION; SEVEN TO TWELVE YEARS INTO THE STANDARDS IMPLEMENTATION PROCESS)

Leadership actions that occur in this stage include the following:

- District leadership publicly articulates a redefinition of student achieve ment that includes multiple assessment opportunities.
- District leadership works with school leaders and teachers to develop a standards based student performance reporting system that reports stu dent achievement on the learning standards rather than only classroom grades.
- Later in this stage, promotion from elementary school to middle school and/or middle school to high school is based on student demonstration of competency of state learning standards, using criteria for student proficiency developed by district personnel and teachers cooperatively.
- Implementation of standards-based graduation requirements requiring student demonstration of competency at a determined level of profi ciency on key assessments or in the presentation of a portfolio of learn ing to a panel of educators may occur late in this stage.

Teacher actions that occur in this stage include the following:

- Teachers begin to articulate the criteria for student demonstration of proficiency on standards and/or benchmarks on a regular basis.

- Rubrics are used consistently to communicate expectations to students.
- Teachers regularly communicate the purpose of the learning standard(s) addressed in each lesson and assessment to students.
- Performance data are regularly shared and tracked by teachers and students to assessment learning and demonstration of proficiency on the standards.
- Teachers begin to provide students with the opportunity to retake as sessments.
- Teachers begin to provide students with preassessment or performance trial opportunities to provide a baseline of performance and to commu nicate the learning expectations to students.
- Teachers regularly create and share classroom assessments based on the standards with peers.
- Later in this stage, teachers solicit and listen to student input in assess ment methods and, finally, instructional methods.

DISTRICT REDEFINITION OF STUDENT LEARNING PERFORMANCE

In the third stage of standards based education implementation, a para digm shift in the opportunities students are given to learn occurs. This shift is initiated by district leaders and is a logical progression in many ways.

Whereas the traditional view of assessment is predominantly summa tive and the goal of classroom instruction is to have a majority, if not all, of the students performing at a desired level at a particular time, the view of educators in the transitional assessment stage becomes predominantly formative and is less time bound. District leaders begin to reframe stu dent performance based on a moral imperative that all students sincerely do need to possess certain knowledge and skills to be successful in their adult lives.

Although the Plainsfield School District was moving into this stage, only the Verde Valley district had accomplished this paradigm shift in its schools. The superintendent of Verde Valley explained, We started off like everybody else did. We started off by doing our curriculum map ping, looking at the state standards, matching the state standards to that mapping and trying to get things horizontally and vertically aligned. Then the next jump from doing that to actually having really standards based instruction was the difficult piece. You have the idea that every child gets the opportunity to move at their own pace and reassess.

Students begin to have more options in how they demonstrate their learning, and, if they do not demonstrate proficiency on a specific stan dard, they are given the opportunity to go back, self assess, and confer ence with their teachers as to what elements of their product did not meet the required criteria and how proficiency would look; do additional study and preparation; and then revise or re create the demonstration of their learning. This is a very different standard operating procedure from the traditional process of a teacher giving an assessment, marking incorrect answers or errors, and then moving on with instruction.

In such a system, the teacher and students can abdicate their responsi bility in the learning process. The teacher can say, I taught it and they just didn t learn it, and the students can say, The teacher did not teach it well enough for me to learn it. In the transitional assessment stage, however, both the teacher and the students are obligated to show mastery of the knowledge and skills required by the standards, no matter how long it takes for the learning to be demonstrated. This obligation is based in a belief that the learning is vital and that belief, as well as the consequent changes in assessment procedures, is conveyed by district leaders.

The assistant superintendent, Abby McDougall, in Verde Valley ex plained that teachers had difficulty with the idea of letting students retake quizzes or tests or revise essays and other assignments. After eight years of trying to help students learn to a proficient level on the state standards, Abby observed that the teachers who were giving multiple opportunities for students to show mastery on assessments were having such success in increasing student achievement as well as increased student motivation. These teachers became models for the teachers who initially felt that such a process would require too much work or lower students responsibility for their learning.

The state assessments and accountability system still served as sum mative guides as to students progress, but the emphasis on having all students perform in the classroom to a proficient level shifted the perspec tive and energy of educators in the district from an external pressure to an internal pressure based on the common value of what students needed out of their schooling experience. Student learning became the focus rather than an annual test score.

Verde Valley s district leaders held a series of open meetings with par ents to discuss student assessment and explain how multiple assessment opportunities would benefit students. In one such meeting, Abby recalls that parents were expressing the view that they felt their child should get a better grade if they mastered the targeted knowledge and skills before other children in their class.

During a public meeting, a student stood up and said, So your kid is smart and gets it the first time. Should I have a chance to get it, too, even if it takes me longer? Why should I only get one shot if what I am learning is really important? What does it matter if I learn it after you do? This observation immediately silenced the parents criticism, Abby observed.
The kids are our best PR people! she added.

Multiple learning opportunities are viewed by the district as more realistic. When parents say that it isn t fair, my kid was the first to get an A, we say that isn t real life. I mean, how many times do you get to take the bar exam before you pass it? How many times do you get to take your pilot s license? You don t just get one chance and then you re done. Life is a constant repeating of opportunities, Stan Evans, the district s superintendent, passionately elaborates. Providing multiple opportunities to demonstrate learning also gives ownership to students. Kids get to de sign how they are going to move forward and demonstrate their progress, he explains.

The district continues to provide professional development for teach ers in the district, sending at least thirty teachers and their principals to national trainings on assessment. These trainings address how teachers can provide multiple means that students can choose from to demonstrate their learning as well as how to manage providing multiple opportunities for students to demonstrate their learning if they do not meet an advanced or proficient criteria level on an assessment.

The teachers also receive additional training, both outside the district and provided by the district, to accurately assess students so that students, teachers, and parents understand exactly what is being assessed, why, and what the criteria are for each level of performance delineated. As teachers became more comfortable and proficient in assessment methods, letter grades seemed inadequate to convey the level of learning that students were demonstrating on assessments.

STANDARDS-BASED GRADING SYSTEM ADOPTION

In traditional grade reporting systems, each student is assigned a letter grade for his or her performance in a subject area over a particular time period, be it a semester or a year. While what that letter grade reports is typically defined by individual teachers with some policy guidance by the district, an A in one classroom might reflect student behavior, such as being late or unprepared for class (which could be anything from not bringing a pencil and paper to not doing one s homework), work habits such as neatness of assignments, and effort in class or on homework.

How much weight is given to any one element is also usually up to the individual teacher. Guskey (2006) calls this hodgepodge grading where a teacher may base a student s grade on one or two things while another teaching in the same school may base a grade on over a dozen different factors. Guskey delineates between product, process, and progress crite ria that are associated with standards based instruction and assessment practices.

Product criteria are usually summative, such as teachers basing a grade on a final test or report. Process criteria take into consideration how students arrived at the final product, such as classroom participation and attendance. Progress criteria grades are based on how much improvement a student demonstrates in a given time period.

None of these methods, however, focuses only on performance of stu dent learning with enough detail to inform the student or parents of the level of performance of the student on a desired learning target or stan dard. Guskey (2006) suggests reporting each factor separately so that the level of student achievement or learning is clear. Tomlinson and McTighe (2006) also suggest that schools provide grades specifically related to the achievement of learning goals, progress toward those goals, and work habits.

Once the different aspects of student performance are separately iden tified, then specific criteria for each can be developed to make letter grades more meaningful. For student achievement of learning targets, the groundwork for accurate reporting of student learning in a standards based education system is laid in stages 1 and 2 with the alignment of curriculum and assessments to specific knowledge and skills targets based on the state learning standards and the subsequent development and use of rubrics by teachers to identify the criteria for proficiency in the demon stration of student learning for each target.

Achievement and progress of students must then be reported as a syn thesis or summary of student performance on learning target assessments. Given the complexity of learning standards, identification of student performance on subareas communicates most clearly what a student has mastered and what he or she still needs to work on.

In the area of writing, this may include an average of performance on a variety of written products across disciplines, provided that the criteria for assessment are uniform across products, as they should be if teachers are creating and sharing common assessments and rubrics. Writing style, expressive language and detail usage, structure or orga nization, and use of standard English conventions may all be included in the criteria.

At least three times each year, parents of students in Verde Valley re ceive a standards based report of student progress in the mail. Progress on standards in the areas of reading and writing, math, science, social studies, health, media skills, and physical education and special subjects such as music, band, choir, or art are indicated on this report for each standard associated with these subject areas.

Progress is indicated using a 1 through 4 point scale with the following explanations of each number on the scale:

1 = Not yet achieved: The proficiency was taught but has not yet been learned.
2 = Partially proficient: The student is able to demonstrate the learning but not consistently.
3 = Proficient: The student demonstrates learning in the proficiency on a consistent basis.
4 = Advanced: The student is proficient and also applies learning to new skills or knowledge.

The report also indicates that items not rated have not yet been assessed. Successful Learner Behaviors are also rated on a scale of consistent, usually, or seldom, with such items as treats others with kindness and respect, resolves problems and conflicts effectively, cooperates on group tasks, and gets to class on time from passing periods included in this list of behaviors.

As Guskey (2006) and others (Ainsworth and Viegut 2006; Tomlinson and McTighe 2006) argue, standards based grade reporting can provide a clear description of student achievement that can be used by students and teachers to differentiate instruction and more effectively support student learning as well as convey student learning more clearly to parents.

In a description of their standards based reporting system on the district website, Verde Valley explains that a Standards Based grading system attempts to hold expectations for students consistent and to separate reporting on student learning from the learner behaviors that impact learning. When parents see a letter grade, they are viewing a highly subjective, inconsistent, and simplified report on student learning. When parents view a performance level, they are viewing a much more accurate picture of what students know and can do (Fox 2009c).

In the transitional assessment stage, district leaders engage in dialogue to answer the important questions regarding assessment, including the following:

- What is the purpose of grades and reporting grades?
- Who will use the reporting information and how?
- How can grades be used to support and advance student learning most effectively?

The district leaders of Verde Valley enlisted the assistance of Guskey in designing a computerized system of recording and reporting student progress on the state s learning standards. While Guskey could provide guidance on how to think about the reporting system, the details were up to them to work out. The system created by the district allows teachers to easily build assessments based on the standards and track the coverage of standards by each assessment and across assessments.

As the new reporting system was developed and revised, the answers to the above questions became clearer and clearer. The district declares, If we didn t believe that a standards based grading system was beneficial for students we wouldn t be making the change! Students and parents are our customers in our educational system and as such, are the first people we consider when evaluating and changing practices (Fox 2009b).

To answer stakeholder questions as to why standards based reporting is better for students, the district outlines the following benefits:

Standards based systems will provide students with clear learning targets.

- Proficiencies for each grade level spell out what students will learn and what they will be tested on, regardless of which teacher they have or which school they attend.
- Proficiencies are derived from documents produced by both the State of Colorado and the school district that describe essential learning for students in all content areas at all grade levels.

Standards based systems will provide students with accurate feedback concerning the learning process.

- Once students understand the learning target or proficiency, they are also made aware of or sometimes will participate in defining how success will be measured and what demonstrations of learning look like. They will know exactly what they need to learn, they will know exactly what the expectation is, and they will work with the teacher to evaluate their work against a set rubric or scoring guide.
- Standards-based systems encourage students to evaluate their own learning when measured against a set scoring guide. Our goal is to help young people develop the ability to evaluate their own work and to make adjustments to that work independently to achieve a successful finished product. The teacher does not decide after the fact what good looks like; that is already decided and understood before a student be gins to produce a product.

Standards based systems recognize that learning is complex and provides for learning to be fixed and time to be flexible.

- Proficiencies for students reflect what students need to master regard less of how long it takes. Because of the individuality of students and the complexity of learning, students learn at different rates and in different ways. Students must demonstrate mastery before moving on to the next set of expectations.
- Just because a grading period ends or a new unit of instruction begins, we do not drop the expectations for students. If students need to know how to add and subtract numbers, we do not give up on that just because it is now time to move on to multiplication and division.

Standards based systems allow students to move ahead in their learning, based on individual need rather than continuing to be taught what they already know.

- Preassessment of student knowledge is the cornerstone of standards-based systems. This practice recognizes the individuality of learners and allows the teacher to provide the right instruction to the right student. If a student is already able to construct a good paragraph, it is important that he or she works on multiple paragraph projects and the skills that accompany that proficiency than to continue to practice what they have already mastered.

Standards based systems require that learning starts where the student is rather than where he or she should be based on an age or grade level.

- Some of our students learn very quickly or, because of a variety of experiences, come to us with a great deal of knowledge already in place. Other students have gaps in their learning because of a variety of circumstances. In some cases, instruction has to focus on filling in the gaps, and in others, instruction focuses on challenging students with new information and learning new skills.

Standards based systems capitalize on the internal motivation for learning.

- Getting excited about learning something new is very motivating. The better we are at something, the more likely we are to want to get better.

If our first attempts at learning result in embarrassment and frustration, we become less and less likely to continue to try. By starting student learning at the appropriate level, by providing students with clear learn ing targets and assessments, and by providing students with as much or as little time to learn as is needed, we can continue to build on student motivation.

- Knowledge of success is motivating. Whether we convey that informa tion to students in the form of letter grades, numbers, or performance levels, the key is that students know they are successful learners. In the end, it matters what students know and can do, not how we report that on a grade card (Fox 2009b).

The values of the district regarding student learning and the assessment of this learning are very clearly articulated. These are explained in the following terms (Fox 2009a):

- Learning, not teaching, becomes the primary focus of teachers.
- Focus on the individual learner and his or her progress in meeting or exceeding the expectation that all students will demonstrate pro ficiency.
- Learning is the nonnegotiable, and time is the variable. Students are allowed to move either faster or slower in their learning as their needs dictate, and the system must accommodate the reality that not all stu dents learn the same thing at the same time in the same way.
- Learning is viewed as a process over time. Grades (performance levels) are not averaged but are evaluated as a natural progression from under standing to mastery.

The emphasis is clearly on student learning, independent of time neces sary, and reflects the paradigm shift characteristics of the transitional assessment stage. Unlike many districts that implement standards based reporting systems only at the elementary level, Verde Valley adopted the standards based reporting system in K 12 over a period of three years. To prevent students from being penalized for the district s unique performance reporting system in scholarship competitions and in college applications, juniors and seniors are provided grade point equivalencies for their performance on the state s standards and a grade point average.

Verde Valley also implemented performance criteria based on the standards for promotion from middle school to high school. Evidence in terms of student work products was gathered together in student portfolios for each learning standard at the eighth grade level. Teams of teachers reviewed each portfolio and the associated performance criteria for each standard before a student could move on to high school. The district was also working on developing similar promotion performance criteria for each grade level through the elementary and middle school grades.

STUDENT INVOLVEMENT IN THE LEARNING PROCESS

While the paradigm shift in the transitional assessment stage comes from district leaders who provide teachers and parents with new knowledge as they engage in a dialogue regarding what students need to learn and be successful, in school and as adults, the role of students in the classroom changes dramatically as well. Many of the experimental efforts that teachers started in the second stage as they concentrated on learning how to collect, analyze, and use data become standard operating procedures regarding instruction and assessment in the classroom.

Preassessment and performance trial opportunities are given on a regular basis for all major assessments. Teachers work together to create all assessments that will impact reporting of student progress on the stan dards, jointly analyzing student data, and holding regular, ongoing profes sional discussions as to how to differentiate their instruction to improve the learning performance of every student.

The role of the student as a partner in using assessments to guide the learning process increases, making the assessment process in particular more student centered than teacher centered, and is a hallmark of the transitional assessment stage. Some of these changes in this stage include student input or development of criteria for all classroom assessments, requiring students to know and understand the desired learning standard and its relevance, and student input on the means of assessment, including multiple methods of demonstrating learning.

Classroom activities in this stage may include the following:

- Student selection of vocabulary words (noted by teachers to be much more difficult than what they would have selected but with higher stu dent mastery on related assessments)
- Student writing of quiz and test questions, indicating the correct answer and how the other incorrect answers reflect lower levels of mastery of the related standard
- Student creation of essay questions or writing prompts and a rubric to grade the written response according to levels of mastery of the related standard
- Student development of projects and related criteria for assessment based on levels of mastery of the related standard

Instructional methods used by the teacher in the classroom remain teacher directed, although student involvement is greater than in a traditional classroom setting. Teachers also still facilitate or guide student input on assessments.

When students in the Verde Valley school district were interviewed, their responses were amazingly consistent, even though they had been selected randomly from among all the students who had returned signed consent and assent forms to participate in an interview. In response to the question of how teachers decide what to teach, every student referred to the state s standards as guiding what their teacher taught them. When asked if their grades really reflected what they had learned, they all agreed that their grades reflected how they did on each standard during that quarter.

It is easy to get a good grade if you just follow the rubric. It s easier for everybody to know what to do, one student explained, adding, If we do bad, we get to retake the test or whatever until we get it right.

When students in Verde Valley were asked how they thought they would do in school that year, students frequently referred to knowing how to do well because of the use of rubrics and teacher feedback on their perfor mance based on the rubric for each assignment. They will hand it back to you and let you know what you have to do differently to get a three or a four, so it is really up to you do to well. While educators may make claims as to increased student ownership of learning through standards based in structional practices, the words of these students support those claims.

CORE ENHANCEMENT ELEMENTS IN
THE TRANSITIONAL ASSESSMENT STAGE

In the third stage of implementation of standards based instructional practices, the core task of creating a learning environment is more fully addressed than in the earlier two stages, as shown in figure 5.1. Students feel safer in taking the risks involved in learning challenging skills and material because they clearly understand the performance that is expected

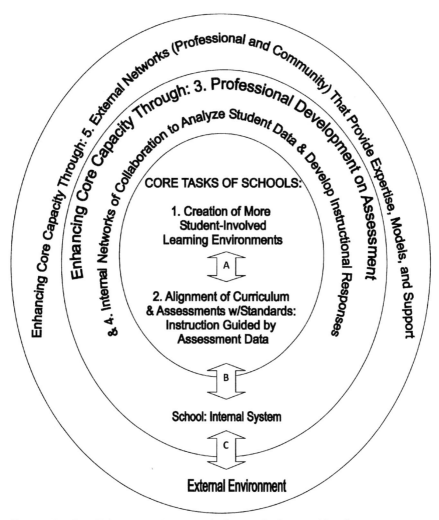

Figure 5.1.　Core-Enhancement Framework Elements in the Transitional Assessment Stage

of them to demonstrate their knowledge and are given multiple opportuni
ties and means to demonstrate their learning.

It is no longer a question of students trying to figure out what they are
supposed to know for a test or how a teacher wants an assignment done
because they have participated in creating the evaluation criteria based on
models of performance at different levels of mastery. The criteria for suc
cess are identified by the students, not just for students, and those criteria
are specific rather than vague.

Assessments in the classroom are further aligned with state learning
standards, with each classroom activity related to specific learning targets
related to the standards. Assessments are constructed first, before instruc
tion is planned, with the learning targets driving both the assessment and
the instruction. Progress is viewed by teachers and students in terms of
learning standards, and information is freely shared among teachers as
well as with students and parents to identify additional learning support
or differentiation of instruction that is needed to increase performance.

Professional development is continued to enhance teacher capacity
specifically related to the assessment process, with ongoing dialogues
to clarify purpose as well as process. Teacher collaboration becomes a
routine part of professional activity with continued development, sharing,
and analysis of student assessments, work, and feedback from peers on
how to enhance instruction for students who are struggling.

Support from parents, as well as outside experts, is imperative in the
transitional assessment stage. For the paradigm shift in viewing student
performance of learning as the focus of all educational effort, independent
of time, parents and teachers need to be reassured that such a change is in
the best interest of students. While district leaders can talk to and teach
parents the benefits of third stage changes, educators need additional
knowledge as well as reassurance. This can come from experts in the
field, such as Guskey and others, or from other practitioners who have
progressed through the transitional assessment stage.

In Verde Valley, teams of teachers visit the district monthly from
across the nation to observe classrooms and learn how district and school
leaders have worked together to move so far along in the implementation
of standards based education. Seeing it done and talking to teachers who
have made the transition and find it beneficial to students, as well as fea
sible for teachers, is a validation and encouragement needed by educators
who are at the brink of the transitional assessment stage.

MOTIVATIONS AND CHALLENGES

Educators at all levels, but particularly at the district level, appear to be motivated by a moral imperative to provide learning opportunities to all students in this stage. While state accountability systems seemed to drive the motivation in earlier stages, student learning became the foremost ideal or value as educators tried to create a learning system that fairly assessed student learning of the standards and fairly provided and sup ported the opportunity for every child to reach a level of proficiency in the transitional assessment stage. Confronted with the challenge of effectively educating all students, including those from low socioeconomic status backgrounds and English language learner students, the old system of ac cepting student failure based on one time assessments and time limits for learning became unacceptable.

As the superintendent of Verde Valley observed, the effort to shed tradition in terms of assessment and performance reporting was a sig nificant challenge, referring to teacher and parent resistance to giving students multiple assessment opportunities and to individually assess and report competency on standards rather than the traditional hodgepodge grading dependent on individual teacher judgment.

This challenge required the investment of professional development resources to advance the skills and knowledge of teachers as well as an investment of time by educational leaders to communicate with and educate parents. The continued and intensified need for teachers to work collaboratively also led to Verde Valley negotiating an additional sixteen workdays for teachers throughout the school year, an investment of both time and monetary resources of the district.

Another challenge that Verde Valley is still trying to respond to is, as promotion to higher grades hinges on a demonstration of mastery of learn ing standards, how will students who do not show adequate mastery at the end of a school year or grade level be supported and instructed to reach the level of mastery? One teacher in the district pondered the difficulties of having students just repeat a grade, anxious about the intellectual, so cial, and emotional impact of such a situation of the student being retained to master the standards as well as the impact such students would have on overall class dynamics.

A possible resolution to this quandary may well lead the Verde Valley into the next stage of standards based education implementation, where

individual student learning demonstration replaces grade level delinea
tions in the educational system.

POINTS TO REMEMBER: MOVING ON TO STAGE 4

For districts to advance from the transitional assessment stage into the
fourth and final stage of being standards led, the following must occur in
this third stage:

- A redefinition of student learning assessment that focuses on student
  mastery of the state s learning standards, independent of time con
  straints
- The provision of multiple opportunities for students to demonstrate
  learning of the standards, including multiple methods or means for
  demonstrating that learning
- Clear and repeated articulation of performance targets to students for
  each assessment
- Use of student assessment data to differentiate instruction in the class
  room on a regular and ongoing basis
- Collaboration among teachers to articulate performance criteria to stu
  dents
- Inclusion of student input in the assessment process
- Clear communication of student performance to students and parents
- Initial identification of essential evidence of student performance and
  related criteria for promotion to the next grade level at significant junc
  tures in the student s education

REFLECTIVE QUESTIONS FOR PRACTITIONERS

Reflective Questions for District Leaders

1. What is the purpose of grades?
2. What is the purpose of communicating student progress?
3. How can the communication of student progress more effectively sup
   port student learning?

4. Who are the stakeholders who need to understand student progress?
5. How can student learning best be communicated to these stakeholders?
6. What are fundamental beliefs about learning and student progress on which the current system of reporting student learning and progress are based?
7. What beliefs would need to change to make the reporting of student progress more effectively support student learning?
8. What additional knowledge and skills do building leaders and teachers need to more effectively report student learning and use assessments to support student mastery of the state learning standards?

Reflective Questions for Building Leaders

1. How do teachers determine grades in your building?
2. What value do the teachers in your building place on student grades? How does this support student learning?
3. How do the use of grades communicate student learning to parents?
4. How could student progress be more effectively communicated to students and parents to support student learning?
5. What is the role of students in the learning process in your school?
6. What means do students in your building have for input into their learning or taking ownership for their learning?
7. What additional knowledge and skills would teachers in your building need to more effectively assess and report student learning in terms of performance on the state s learning standards to support student mastery of those standards?

Reflective Questions for Teacher Leaders

1. What is the purpose of grades?
2. How do you determine student grades?
3. What do grades communicate regarding student learning to parents and to students?
4. How could you more effectively communicate student performance related to the state learning standards to both students and parents?
5. What do you do to give ownership of the learning process to students in your classroom?

6. What could you do in your classroom to increase student involvement and ownership in the learning process?

7. What knowledge or skills do you think would help you to 1) more accurately communicate student learning and 2) increase student in volvement in the learning process?

8. What products or evidence document a student s mastery of standards at a grade level that indicate that a student is ready to move on to the next grade level?

PORTRAIT OF A TEACHER IN A LATE TRANSITIONAL ASSESSMENT STAGE SCHOOL

Michael Sparks has been teaching eighth grade language arts at Pearsall Middle School in the Verde Valley district for four years, having taught one year in another district before coming to the Verde Valley commu nity. His teaching is guided by the philosophy that schooling should try to give all kids the skills they re going to need for life, so instead of just practicing, I try to have them participate in their society by the things that they write in my classroom. He feels that the state s learning standards give him guidance as for what to shoot for in terms of the kids without taking the freedom away from the teacher.   They give me freedom be cause they say, This is what you have to do, now do whatever you want to get them there, Michael explains.

While he feels that the standards based reporting system is a move in the right direction, he feels that it needs to be revised to be more easily understood by parents and even students. Parents learn more about what their students are doing during the four expo nights that the school hosts each year. At each grade level, students may present different products to display their learning.

At the eighth grade level this year, the students have compiled port folios that will be assessed at the end of the year to determine if they have demonstrated mastery of the standards to a level sufficient to move on to high school. The parent really sees what the kids are do ing. They see what knowledge they have to have. . . . It s neat because the parents are starting to be awed at what they re doing, he explains enthusiastically.

In discussing student assessments, Michael says that he and his col
leagues still crank the numbers on the state and district assessments at
the beginning of each year, so the kids know their scores and they know
what proficient is, partially proficient, and we talk about what their areas
of weakness are. We have a lot of teacher days where we can sit down
and talk and aggregate data from our own tests and say which sections of
this am I teaching effectively and which am I not. We assess ourselves and
move forward, he says of his work with other teachers on making sense
of assessment data that they gather from common assessments.

Michael stresses that much of the learning of teachers regarding assess
ment has come from these discussions, where they are learning about
what standards based really means. It s a philosophy change. It s a totally
different way of thinking about education, although he also notes that a
lot of professional development is continually provided by or through the
district to help teachers think differently about the educational process.

It is still the professional dialogue that he feels has been of most value
to him. We have a lot of discussions about how to assess and what the
function of the report card is and the difference between practice and as
sessment, Michael explains, but how that translates into making learning
meaningful and real in his classroom remains his primary responsibility
as a teacher.

Michael views his role in the classroom as a resource for them to gain
the skills they need but likes to see students becoming increasingly active
in their own education. They become cognizant of the things that they re
learning, what they know and what they don t know, and are proactive in
getting help for things that they need assistance with. In his classroom,
that means he adamantly refuses to let a student take a zero for an assign
ment he or she didn t have completed on time.

Using a favorite song selected by each student to exemplify poetic ele
ments, Michael encourages everyone in the class to come to a local cof
feehouse for a poetry jam the following week and share the poem that they
are working on in class that day. After checking each students progress
and giving suggestions on adding more details or visuals to the poetry
packets that they had developed, referencing the poetry rubric as he gives
his feedback, Michael asks everyone to pick the best or most meaningful
poem that they had written, practice reading it aloud with a partner, and
then read their selection to the class.

The first student to share, Lon, used a format that the teacher had in
troduced a week or so before based on relating an emotional experience
or feeling to an object. Lon compared himself to a hammock, stretched
between reality and imagination. After two more poems were shared,
Michael shared one he had written and asked for feedback from the class.

The final poem of the period was authored by Antonio but read by an
other female student because Antonio felt uncomfortable reading in front
of the group. The poem spoke of feeling alone and trying to do the right
thing while being treated badly and wanting to find freedom and escape.
The reader of the poem, as well as the teacher and many other students
in the class, agreed that the poem was awesome, and Antonio shyly
beamed.

The classroom environment was supportive but challenging academi
cally, using student interests as the venue for learning and capitalizing on
student input into the form and content of their poetic products. Sharing
their work in a venue outside the classroom strengthened the real world
link that Michael values as well. Although the standards guided what was
being learned and a rubric was used to assess student work, the learning
process in no way felt standardized or rote, just focused and authentic.

Chapter Six

Stage 4: Standards-Led Education—A New System

**STANDARDS-LED STAGE (THREE YEARS'
AVERAGE DURATION; THIRTEEN TO FIFTEEN
YEARS INTO THE IMPLEMENTATION PROCESS)**

Leadership actions that occur in this stage include the following:

- District leadership publicly articulates a redefinition of the role of school in student learning.
- Grade level promotion is based on student demonstrations of competency of standards.
- Later in this stage, age level grades are eliminated.

Teacher actions that occur in this stage include the following:

- Purpose of learning and standards are clearly and consistently articulated to all students.
- Student input is solicited regarding instructional methodology.
- Student input is clearly evident and sought in instructional and assessment processes.
- Instruction is fully guided by student performance assessment data.
- All students have multiple opportunities and methods of demonstrating competency of the standards.

ELIMINATION OF AGE-BASED STUDENT GROUPING

Of the eight school districts studied, only Verde Valley is at the brink of entering the final stage of standards based education implementation to a truly standards led system. This stage is marked by a rethinking of how students progress through the public education system.

As the superintendent of Verde Valley explains, We still have pieces of a system that doesn t work well together. It makes no sense to have a third grade, a fourth grade, and so forth. When you re in a traditional system, you are eight years old, so you are in a particular grade. But in a truly standards led system, what you are learning is defined by what you have already learned and need to learn next, not your age.

Another large urban school district in the state that this study was conducted in is also entering this stage, laying the groundwork to remove age based, developmental based grade levels and exchanged them for academic, achievement based levels, following in the Chugach School District s success in Alaska in the 1990s. The use of academic develop mental levels in place of age determined grade levels in a standards led education system is a logical extension of monitoring and reporting stu dent progress on learning standards.

In a standards based education system, students progress through lev els of proficiency in each subject area with the assistance of teachers. Groupings would still occur but would be more flexible and responsive to individual student learning needs. If a student progresses very rapidly through the lower learning standards in a subject, he or she can move on to a higher or more complex set of learning standards in that subject without having to wait for the end of the year or the appropriate birthday. Each student has, in essence if not in fact, an individualized learning plan where teachers monitor learning and provide additional instruction and practice as needed.

Given the American public school system s goal of educating every student to his or her maximum potential, this sounds like an ideal system, although how this can be done might draw criticism in terms of practi cality. The current Response to Intervention model is, in many ways, a step toward such individualization of instruction although not intended to disrupt the age based grade structure of public schools. However, there are schools that have accomplished the structural change of replacing age determined grade levels with performance based groupings with great success that can serve as models.

The Chugach School District adopted performance based instructional groupings ten years ago and continues working with a coalition of sev enteen schools under the auspices of the Alaskan Quality Schools Model (AQSM). The Bering Strait School District, part of the AQSM network, is one of several Alaskan districts in the coalition that are working in partnership with the Alaska Staff Development Network, the Reinvent ing Schools Coalition, and the Bill & Melinda Gates Foundation with the goal of enabling all students to meet high standards. As the Reinventing Schools Coalition website proclaims, Innovative learning is the constant, time is the variable (http://www.chugachschools.com/standards_based _system/shared_vision/index.html).

Schools using AQSM structure the learning environment using

flexible grouping strategies that have students of various ages working together based on their skill mastery in our curriculum standards. Some classes in core content areas are grouped by ability, such as Reading and Math. Others are usually more heterogeneous in composition.

Students advance through the nine Content Area standards at their own individual developmental pace, aiming to meet or exceed the graduation level in each content area. Each content area has between five and twelve levels of standards that students progress through. Each one also has an identified level that is considered the minimum required for graduation.

There is a mastery learning component involved since district wide assessments are used to document student skill attainment in each of the standards before they are allowed to move to the next level. (http://wiki .bssd.org/index.php/Stuff_for_new_hires_about_the_model)

The content areas taught and assessed in the AQSM include career skills, cultural awareness, life skills, math, reading, science, social science, tech nology, and writing.

While the critics of standards based education movement often cite the decreased emphasis on life skills and social development, the inclusion of these areas of child development do not have to be excluded from a standards based model of education, as evidenced by AQSM. The content models need to simply reflect the areas valued by the society supporting the educational system.

Built on the Baldrige model of school improvement that was advanced by many state and national business organizations in the 1990s, AQSM goes beyond the continuous improvement of language and data monitor ing that bogged down many schools that had experimented with the Bal drige model and targets the essential elements of learning and schooling.[1] The AQSM includes seven elements that are common to many recipes for school reform, such as development of a shared vision, leadership, stan dards, effective instruction, multiple assessments, meaningful reporting, and continuous improvement.

The difference is in the details perhaps. The development of a vi sion includes extensive community input and consideration of cultural responsiveness. District mission statements and strategic action plans, locally relevant school project and unit design, and thematic units are all aligned with the shared vision. Student assessment includes multiple measures, methods, and opportunities. These include skill based, ana lytic (assessing the ability to apply knowledge and skills), contextual (assessing the application of knowledge and skills in a real world con text), and self assessments in addition to state and national standardized exams.

While effective instructional methods do not eliminate some drill and practice required to master basic facts, practical application, interaction, and use of real life scenarios are emphasized. An electronic, standards based student performance reporting system called the Data Analysis and Reporting Toolkit (DART) is used and is electronically available to parents and students as well as educators.

These efforts have resulted in a tremendous increase in the quantity and quality of communication between the schools and their communities. Students are much more engaged in their learning and their participation and confidence has increased. Student achievement indicators (standard ized test scores, % of students engaged in post secondary programs, etc.) have skyrocketed (http://wiki.bssd.org/index.php/Stuff_for_new_hires _about_the_model).

Various aspects of the model include the following, according to the Bering Strait School District wiki page (http://wiki.bssd.org/index.php/ Stuff_for_new_hires_about_the_model):

- Increased achievement in core content areas
- Greatly expanded, coordinated staff development in all district programs
- Dispersed leadership for reform in a horizontal dimension
- Widely adopted tools for collaborative work over distance
- Reduced dependence on proprietary curriculum materials and vendor driven programs
- Organizational commitment to collecting and using data for decision making
- Dramatically reduced teacher turnover rates
- Significantly improved ability to recruit and retain high quality educators

The emphasis on student achievement of standards, multiple assess ment methods and opportunities, and the elimination of age based educa tional groupings converge to create a student centered learning environ ment. (This environment also appears to appeal to the educators in the system from the turnover data reported.) The Chugach district posts this comparison between the original district system and the system that is now in place (http://www.chugachschools.com/standards_based_system/ shared_vision/index.html):

Original System	Twenty First Century System
Learning needs not met	Individualized learning plans for every student
Credit or seat time	Standards based system
Graded system	Ungraded system
Disconnected reporting system	P 14 standards report card
Traditional assessments contextual	Skills based, analytical, self , and assessments
Textbook curriculum	Standards based curriculum
Poor transition system	Electronic P 14 student profile
No school to life plan	Comprehensive school to life plan
Institutionally centered	Student centered

For those who doubt that a standards led educational system is practical and effective, perhaps they should plan a trip to Alaska and visit Chugach, Bering Strait, and other schools using the AQSM elements in their districts.

STUDENT-CENTERED LEARNING SYSTEMS

While the elimination of age based grade levels is the most dramatic structural change that marks the standards led stage, the adoption of a truly student centered learning philosophy is of equal importance to sup port student engagement and achievement.

A district in a western state moving into this stage lists the following on its website as hallmarks of their learner centered standards based edu cational model (http://www.sbsadams50.org/content/component/content/article/77.html):

- Classroom shared vision and code of conduct
- Students are partners in teaching-learning cycle
- Students and teachers are collaborative
- Students own their learning
- Students monitor and assess their own learning
- Students provide feedback through tools and processes

These six norms of a standards led classroom make the instructional process student centered and allow students to take full advantage of a standards based educational system by increasing engagement and mo tivation. This philosophy is seen as complementing the elimination of age based grade groupings in the district.

In Sarason s (2002) *Educational Reform: A Self Scrutinizing Memoir*, several criticisms of the traditional educational system are presented that can be addressed in a standards led system that is student centered. By having students help develop classroom visions and codes of conduct, students assume an active role in the governing and maintenance of the classroom environment, teaching children and young adults social skills as well as how to actively participate in a social system that would lay the groundwork for functioning as an active citizen in a democracy.

Giving students options in their learning process, whether it is the choice of a problem to study in an interdisciplinary unit or selecting a means of assessment that capitalizes on a student s interests or talents, increases the possibility that the curiosity and questioning that children bring to school will grow rather than decrease, ideally extending into the concept of lifelong learning that populates many districts mission statements but is sometimes difficult to find in the traditional system of teacher centered classroom instruction.

Students, as with learners of any age, have basic needs for the learning process to be enacted. Some of these include the following:

- The need to feel as though they can do what is being asked of them; otherwise, they will become frustrated and eventually give up.
- Be able to monitor how they are doing so that they can make changes and improve.
- See personal relevance in what they are trying to learn.

In a student centered classroom, students are clearly told what they need to do and why it is relevant (in terms of real life scenarios) and are given an abundance of feedback from each assessment to tell them how they are doing and what they need to do differently. This is very differ ent from the traditional presentation of information because the teacher says it is important and guessing what the important information is that will be assessed and what doing it right looks like. Students need to feel a sense of control as well as purpose about their learning to be engaged and work to learn to their maximum potential.

Stiggins (2007) explains the snowball effect of student success in schools as either an upward spiral in which, if there is early evidence that they are succeeding, what begins to grow in them is a sense of hope fulness and an expectation of more success, in turn fueling enthusiasm and the motivation to try hard or a downward spiral if the evidence suggests to students that they are not succeeding, what can then begin to grow in them is a sense of hopelessness and an expectation of more failure. This can rob them of the confidence they need to take the risk of trying to learn more. So they stop trying and stop learning, which in turn leads to more failure (19).

Covington (1993) went into great detail about the impact of the combina tion of attributes such as high and low effort and ability on a student s per ception of success and actual success. As Stiggins goes on to explain, how ever, this does not mean that students should receive only positive feedback but rather that assessments used in the classroom should clearly help both the teacher and the student identify where a student is at in the acquisition of knowledge and skills and what the next steps are to advance that process.

Feedback must be authentic for it to be meaningful to a learner. Empty praise and positive strokes may make a student feel good for a little while but does nothing to promote learning and the self esteem that comes from learning.

Many teachers in the districts studied expressed a fear of giving up con trol of the learning process to students. While the teacher still remains as a vital guide and facilitator of the learning process as well as providing struc ture to the learning experience, student centered instruction does require a significant shift in how teachers view students in the learning process.

Dr. Paul Baker, an esteemed professor of educational administration at Illinois State University, once observed that all the concepts associated with adult learning or andragogy were simply good instructional prac tices, regardless of the age of the learner. Some of these principles include the following:

- A valuing of personal experiences and perspectives (as well as scaffold ing based on those experiences and understandings)
- A readiness to learn when it is personally relevant
- A need to be involved in the planning of instruction
- A need for some degree of self-direction

If these principles can be applied to adult learning situations   which they have for decades in many successful workshops, seminars, and graduate courses   then the same can be done in public school classrooms. Teachers need to come to view their students as potentially responsible and receptive learners who are active partners in their learning and not just passive receptacles. Instruction must be redefined as something done with students, not just done to students.

Creating student centered classroom learning environments means that teachers must change their philosophy and practice of teaching from what most have experienced in their own education. The philosophical and ped agogical characteristics of student involvement in a traditional classroom and a student centered classroom, as well as the two intermediary stages in which teachers slowly release some control of learning to students, are outlined in table 6.1.

It is hoped that, as more schools move into the standards led stage, teacher preparation institutions will focus on the philosophy and practices

Table 6.1. Traditional to Student-Centered Philosophical and Classroom Practices Evolutionary Stages

Stage	Philosophical Characteristics	Classroom Practices
Traditional	Learning is linear	Instruction is teacher centered
	Information is given to students	Assessment is summative
	Learning is a function of ability	Formative feedback is minimal
	Assessment is viewed as independent of instruction	Instructional tasks are determined by external forces (i.e., district curriculum and/or texts)
		Emphasis of assessment and reporting is on ability rather than effort and progress
		Assessment tasks are determined by external forces (i.e., district and/or texts)
		Student learning is reported in terms of performance on summative assessments
		Student learning is reported in terms of letter grades or percentages
Transitional	Learning is linear	Instruction is teacher centered
	Students construct knowledge	Articulation to students of learning targets
	Learning is a function of a combination of ability and effort	Some formative use of summative assessments through rubrics to provide feedback
	Awareness of learning targets	Assessment tasks are determined by external forces (i.e., district and/or texts, with teacher revisions)
	Awareness of appropriate methods of assessing learning targets	Student learning is reported in terms of performance on summative assessments
	Awareness of the use of formative assessments	Student learning is reported in terms of letter grades or percentages with supplemental information on individual progress
		Development of some teacher-generated classroom assessments

continued

Table 6.1. *Continued*

Stage	Philosophical Characteristics	Classroom Practices
Student involved	Learning is nonlinear Students construct knowledge	Instruction is teacher centered Students are aware of learning targets and characteristics of accomplishment of those targets (i.e., through the use of rubrics or models)
	Learning is a function of effort and progress	Some use of formative assessments with multiple opportunities for students to correct/perfect their performance through feedback
	Importance of assessment in the instructional process	Instruction and assessment includes student involvement with a great deal of teacher guidance
	Value of formative assessment and feedback to student learning	Student learning is reported in terms of summative assessment achievement and individual progress
		Alternative grading marks or explanations are used in addition to more traditional grades or percentage delineations
Student centered	Learning is nonlinear Students construct knowledge	Instruction is student centered Students are fully aware of learning targets and understand the practical need for each target
	Learning is a function of effort and progress	Instruction is student involved and instruction is coconstructed with teacher guidance
	Highest value placed of formative assessment and feedback to guide student learning	All assessments are used formatively; multiple assessment methods and opportunities are available to all students in demonstrating learning
	Assessment is viewed as a fundamental part of the learning process	Student learning is reported in terms of progress toward identified targets instead of letter grades or percentages
	Students have a participative role in constructing and analyzing data from assessments	All classroom assessments are developed with student input and analyze their own performance data to guide their learning goals and plans
	Learning is measured not by units of time but by performance of learning standards	Age-based student groupings are eliminated and replaced by performance-based student groupings with individualized learner plans that are self-paced

necessary for teachers to successfully create, support, and function in a student centered classroom environment.

MOTIVATIONS AND CHALLENGES

The motivation of the Verde Valley district to establish performance based student groupings is the logical extension of basing student learning experiences and performance reporting on mastery of learning standards as well as the desire to support every student s success. The motivation for the schools in Alaska to adopt AQSM and the western school to elimi nate age based student groupings stems from serious achievement gaps in performance between students of different socioeconomic and racial categories on state assessments.

In a standards led educational system, school structures and instruc tional methods are designed in response to and fully aligned with the achievement of students on the learning standards, allowing instruction to be more responsive to and supportive of student learning, regardless of what at risk factors a student might be identified as having.

The challenges vary, influenced largely by local support and resources. Because creation of a standards led educational system does require a philosophical change, district leaders must be outstanding communicators to parents and the community, perhaps more so in this stage than in the earlier three stages because this stage does require a structural change in how students are educated.

The building of support through dialogue can serve many beneficial purposes for schools. Discussion forums can answer parent and taxpayer questions, become a venue of sharing supportive research, and provide opportunities for educational leaders to articulate how a change will benefit students and the community. Such dialogue can also become an essential element in building political support that can impact the district s resources.

In the Verde Valley district, the high income tax base of the com munity, coupled with high expectations for student success held by the community, provided the district with the resources to access national experts, to send large groups of educators every year to national train ings, and to add sixteen days to the school calendar for greater teacher collaboration.

Not all districts can afford to do any or all of those things, which can partially explain why more schools studied had not yet advanced to the final standards led stage. However, when confronted with a crisis that is properly framed and communicated by educational leaders, communities may be more financially supportive of public schools on a local basis, and educational leaders can become more creative as well.

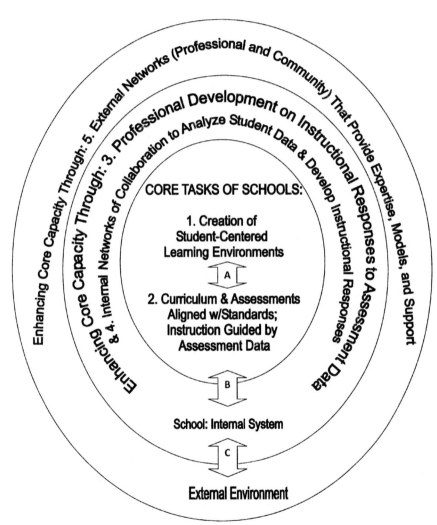

Figure 6.1.   Core-Enhancement Framework Elements in the Standards-Led Stage

Educational leaders in such schools as the Alaskan consortium sought additional outside resources and creatively managed available resources to make the changes called for in a standards led system. Resources can be a challenge, but the response to that challenge depends on the determination of educational leaders who value the potential outcomes of a standards led educational system.

In summary, a standards led system can promote the development of more active and responsible, as well as knowledgeable, skilled, and motivated, citizens. Given the success of the Alaskan consortium schools, cultural awareness and social skills can be nurtured in such a system and narrow the achievement gap between poor and minority students and affluent White students. Given these possible outcomes, it is hoped that a shortage of resources will not prevent such a change from occurring in American public schools.

CORE ENHANCEMENT ELEMENTS IN THE STANDARDS-LED STAGE

In the fourth and final standards led stage, all internal and external structures of the core enhancement framework are fully engaged and coherently aligned to support student learning, as shown in figure 6.1. The classroom environment is student centered, supporting the development of student responsibility, motivation, and progress toward mastery of the learning standards. The curriculum is based on the standards and assessments at all levels of the system, particularly the classroom; monitors student progress on the standards; and provides meaningful feedback to teachers and data that guide instruction.

Teachers collaborate on a regular schedule to examine and use student data to guide instruction. Professional development is regularly provided to increase teachers skills regarding student assessment, use of assessment data, and development of responsive instructional experiences and opportunities. Partnerships are developed and strengthened with external experts and institutions, and the community is aware of and involved in educational processes, all with the goal of supporting student achievement.

POINTS TO REMEMBER

In the standards led stage, the following occurs:

- Restructuring of the school system from age-based student groupings to performance based ability groupings
- Adoption of student-centered instructional methods that include student collaboration with teachers in the teaching and learning cycle, student ownership of learning, student monitoring and assessment of their own learning, student feedback on the learning process, and student input on social norms and conduct

Since the only constant is change, what lies beyond this stage is unclear. Many of the most recent initiatives, such as P 16 alignment and work readiness standards, fit within the structure of standards led education described in this chapter. Greater involvement of parents, professionals, and community members also fits in this structure but perhaps in roles or as a part of the formal structure of public schools that are yet undefined or undeveloped. Technology, with the potential for varied formats and ven ues for learning, will perhaps open the next stage in what a standards led educational system might look like to support the learning and achieve ment of all students.

REFLECTIVE QUESTIONS FOR PRACTITIONERS

Reflective Questions for District Leaders

1. What would the role of a teacher be in a performance based classroom?
2. How would student progress be monitored and supported in a perfor mance based educational system?
3. What would performance based student grouping look like, and how would students progress from one group to another?
4. What knowledge and skills will teachers need to successfully support the learning of all students in a performance based educational system?
5. How will you communicate the need for performance based student groupings to parents and to other relevant stakeholders?

Reflective Questions for Building Leaders

1. What is your understanding of the district s vision of the role of a teacher in a performance based classroom?
2. What is your understanding of how student progress will be monitored and supported in a performance based educational system?
3. What is your understanding of how students will be grouped and prog ress in a performance based educational system?
4. How will you assess teacher effectiveness and provide supportive feedback to teachers in a performance based educational system?
5. How can you best support teachers in a performance based educational system?

Reflective Questions for Teacher Leaders

1. How would you deliver instruction in a performance based classroom?
2. How would students work together to support each other s learning in a performance based classroom?
3. How would students be transitioned into and out of a performance based classroom?
4. How would individual student performance be monitored and sup ported in a performance based classroom?
5. What additional knowledge and skills will you need to successfully support the learning of all students in a performance based class room?

PORTRAIT OF A TEACHER IN
A STANDARDS-LED SCHOOL

Stan Dardsled is in his fourth year of teaching at Achievement Middle School.[2] His philosophy is that his role as a teacher is to support and guide the learning of all his students as they work on understanding and show ing proficiency in the language arts standards adopted by his state as well as helping students to demonstrate proficiency on other state standards, including cultural awareness, social development, and standards in other disciplines.

Stan believes that, given time and appropriate models, feedback, and instruction, every student in his classroom will demonstrate the learning necessary to move on to the next performance level. Stan firmly believes that it is up to him to tap into the talents and interests of his students to show them how language arts can improve their life experiences, both now and in the future, as citizens, workers, and human beings.

The students in Stan s room, ranging in age from twelve through fif teen, are peer critiquing the poetry that they have written based on the rubric that the students developed after reading a variety of acclaimed poems brought in by Stan and also collected by the students. Each student will select a sample of his or her poetry to be reviewed by Stan, and, when he agrees that the selected poems demonstrate proficiency on the rubric, the students will decide how they will present their poems at the spring Academic Achievement Fair.

At the fair, each will display his or her electronic learning portfolios and artifacts. Some students plan to visually present their poems, drawing on their artistic or technological skills, while others plan to set their poems to music and create a video recording of the performance of their poems. The students are proud to share their best work and anxious to create ef fective presentations that will engage others at the fair.

The students will work in small groups to assist each other with the elec tronic display of their products according to the norms of cooperation and support for learning of all that guides their interactions in Stan s classroom, which were agreed on by the students and are reviewed (and revised as necessary in a democratic manner) on a regular basis. All the students will develop a rationale as to how the format they selected supports the mean ing or purpose of each poem. These artifacts will be digitally added to their electronic portfolios, along with evidence of proficiency on the standards they have accomplished since the fall fair in each competency area.

NOTES

1. W. Edwards Deming, the creator of the Baldrige model of continuous im provement, specifically said that his system should not be applied to education.

2. This is, admittedly, an idealistic scenario but one that is surely worth pursuing.

Chapter Seven

Implications for Change

With the imminent adoption of national language arts and mathematics standards by forty eight of the fifty states (Phillips and Wong 2010), the stages described in the preceding chapters may serve as a guide to districts and schools as they make sense of what it means to have a standards led educational system. To assess the stage of standards based implementation in your school or district, a graphic depiction of what occurs in each stage is included in appendix A, followed by a self review assessment instrument in appendix B.

If state or national curricula evolve from the current educational standards movement, such efforts could be used as guides to support student learning, if constructed properly. Local flexibility and instructional choices should complement such guidelines to support the community contexts of learners and the learning environment.

As can be seen from the experiences of schools discussed in this book, basing an educational system on standards implies more than just alignment of curriculum, assessments, and instruction. For such a system to reach its full potential, the view of the student as a learner must change, as must how teachers structure classrooms to involve and engage students.

THE ROLE OF EDUCATION POLICY

Many educators have worried that standards mean standardization of instruction, which could narrow learners experiences and possibly turn more students off to school and learning. Standardization of instruction and all the associated problems of low student engagement are real risks if accountability systems do not adopt a growth model in measuring and reporting student achievement and school effectiveness.

Standards based education could quickly become the means of disas sembling the American public school system rather than reforming it if federal and state accountability systems use only rigid methods to mea sure student achievement and view reorganization of schools as the way to fix failing schools. It may be difficult for educators to embrace reform that is framed only in a negative context or where penalties are the only motivation for innovative changes to the system of schooling.

Given the alarming information of how charter schools educate lower percentages of minority students, students of poverty, English language learner (ELL) students, and students with special needs (Miron et al. 2010), reorganization of failing public schools into segregated charter schools will not increase the educational opportunities or potential of these students but only widen the achievement gap between them and affluent White students. The arguments made by Miller (1995) of the danger to society of permitting and perpetuating an achievement gap still ring true today regarding both minority and poor students.

No society can remain healthy and productive if it does not support and utilize the knowledge and productivity of a large percentage of the population. This is particularly critical as minority student numbers grow and become the majority of society. History holds many examples of what becomes of societies that discriminate through inequity of opportunity toward the majority of its members. While charter schools can properly serve as a research and development venue for public education, segre gated charter schools cannot become the de facto American public school system.

Change is a learning process, and the districts, schools, and educators described in this book learned at a rate that was necessary to meet their needs, admittedly motivated by state accountability pressures and pending sanctions but also mindful of what would best serve students. As with any learning process, some things must be understood and practiced before other ideas can make sense and other skills developed. It is assistance in the form of high quality professional development that federal and state education agencies need to provide to struggling districts and schools for sustainable and equitable change to take place.

In the early twenty first century, education policy has concentrated predominantly on the issue of alignment of curriculum to standards, with alignment of assessments and instruction following as a logical conse quence. Coherent and comprehensive standards in the core subject areas, particularly if based on national model standards, would certainly help ensure that every student, regardless of what state he or she resides in, is exposed to and assisted in learning the essential knowledge needed to be a functioning member of society.

The change to a standards led system must then be an evolutionary process that does not concentrate only on the alignment of curriculum, assessments, and instruction with standards. As important as alignment is, the development of a learning environment is the other and equally important core task of schools and educators. Both changes require stable leadership that does indeed lead changes, not just maintain the status quo, while informing and gaining the support of parents, students, and com munity stakeholders.

Students are not widgets, of course, and learning requires the engage ment of the learner and the motivation to learn. Learning is something an individual does, not something that is done to a person. For students to master the skills and knowledge contained in subject matter standards, the creation of a student centered learning environment is essential. It is this shift that requires intensive educator training and dialogue to be suc cessful.

Education policy in the early twenty first century has also relied almost exclusively on sanctions for schools that do not show adequate student progress rather than providing supportive guidance and instruction re garding how to better teach students. The possible shift in emphasis from highly qualified teachers who know their subject matter to *effective* teach ers who are able to convey their knowledge and assist student learning is a welcomed and much needed change. As the effectiveness of teachers is more closely scrutinized, it is hoped that more of the knowledge and skills associated with instructional effectiveness will be taught to preservice and practicing teachers as well as used in evaluating the classroom practices of teachers.

An investment in professional development and learning at any stage of an educator s career is an investment in capacity building, affecting every student in each teacher s classroom. It is this investment in the growth of teachers that has been largely missing from education policy because of the potential cost of such an investment. Providing opportunities for teachers to learn what they can and must do to effectively teach students the standards requires time and resources, but it is a vital and necessary investment in student achievement.

Current and future research on effective teaching practices can assist in targeting professional development content to best utilize both the time of teachers and the financial resources of education agencies. If the achieve ment of all students is truly the goal of the American public education system, this should then be viewed as a nonnegotiable investment.

Based on the experiences of the schools studied, professional develop ment at both the preservice and the in service level should be provided to teachers and to principals who are to lead the instructional process in the following areas:

- Collaboration protocols
- Alignment of curriculum with standards
- Development of classroom student performance criteria for each stan dard and competencies contained in each standard
- Analysis and use of student performance data
- Development of instructional responses to student performance data
- Development of common classroom assessments
- Development and use of rubrics to assess student performance
- Methods of providing effective feedback to students on performance related to the standards
- Methods of involving students in rubric and assessment development and use
- Methods of supporting student self-monitoring and analysis of progress, including development of metacognitive skills
- Methods of involving students in establishing social norms that fa cilitate multiage student groupings and a performance based learning environment

The overarching theme of the professional growth needed is assessment literacy. Educators who are to lead standards based districts, schools, and classrooms must become assessment literate in order to design classroom assessments that can be used to authentically monitor student learning and provide meaningful data and feedback to teachers and students. Edu cators must know how to respond to assessment data with appropriate instructional strategies and involve students in both the assessment and the instructional process.

In addition to increasing instructional effectiveness, these skills will build the capacity of teachers to be effective players in the accountability arena by being proactive and open about school performance data, and by being able to hold their own in the contentious debate about the uses and misuses of achievement data in an era of high stakes testing (Fullan 2001b, 127), hopefully influencing future education policy development and implementation to support the achievement of all students.

The schools that advanced into the third and fourth stages of standards based education implementation in this book addressed both of the core tasks of schools: the creation of a student involved or student centered learning environment and the alignment of curriculum, assessments, and instruction with learning standards. Instead of a standardization of the learning experience, more opportunities for individualized learning were created for students in these schools as a part of a student centered learn ing environment.

If education policy supports the learning of teachers in both of these areas, the observed time span required for organizational learning in each of the implementation stages may be shortened, increasing the educational opportunities for more students, sooner rather than later. The adoption of a standards led education system, such as the system used by the Alaskan school consortium described in chapter 6, appears to hold great potential for increasing the achievement of students from all socioeconomic back grounds, languages, and racial groups and narrowing the achievement gap that has doggedly plagued American public schools.

CHALLENGES

Traditional Structures

Institutions are slow to change, and all the education reform efforts from the 1950s through the present bear witness to that resistance to change.

The often cited example of a student s grandparents visiting a modern classroom and recognizing many of the instructional methods used, as well as how instructional time is structured, is all too frequently an accu rate depiction of how little the instructional process has changed. Students may be using PowerPoint presentations, but the book report format is the same. Lectures still dominate classes in the later grades, just as work sheets (even if they are completed on a laptop) also persist.

While none of these activities are bad or inherently ineffective in pro moting student learning, the changes outlined in the standards led stage require both educators and society to examine and embrace new structure and roles for students, specifically performance based student grouping and the development of student centered classroom environments. This first requires educational leaders to develop a clear vision of the new structure and roles based on a detailed definition of what standards based education is in practice.

Leaders must then formulate a plan to communicate that vision to the appropriate stakeholders, providing the education that each group needs to successfully participate in making the vision a reality. This includes an understanding of educational benefits for students by parents and educa tors and the provision of training to principals and teachers to function effectively. Educating stakeholders and building support for changes in the educational system is critical in the process of reform. Leaders who do not build this support frequently find their leadership opportunities to be short lived.

Moving Targets

Whether it is a revision of state standards, the adoption of national core standards, or a new emphasis on college and work readiness, cultural awareness, social development, or technological competency, learning standards will always and should always change. Educators may lament this as trying to hit a moving target, but as society changes, so must the preparation of young people in our schools if, as graduates, they are to function effectively within that society.

Although revisions to standards and the addition of new competency ar eas will require a realignment of curriculum, assessments, and instruction, the process of education would not be disrupted in a standards led system that is designed for individual mastery of knowledge and skills. Such a standards led system would be more responsive to changes in student preparation needs because it would already be addressing and responding to individual student learning needs.

Resources

Time and professional development are the two investments needed for the implementation of standards led educational practices, and both have dollar signs attached to them. Districts can reallocate current professional development resources to target the areas listed previously to prepare their school leaders and teachers to function effectively in a standards based educational system, but, given the inequity of resources of schools within states and among states across the nation, the playing field is not a level one, based on current methods of funding public education.

Often the most resource poor districts serve students with the most learn ing challenges. While federal funds may provide additional resources to these schools, local funding of such schools that are dependent on property taxes are often inadequate. The resources available to such schools are often inadequate to support the student learning structures necessary to accelerate students achievement to a proficient level, let alone support the necessary teacher training required to address student learning challenges.

While some states have been successful in getting courts to recognize these inequities and legislatures to adopt more equitable funding methods, it had not solved the problem for the majority of schools in America. The argument that, if all students are held to the same standard of perfor mance, it is a state s obligation to provide equitable resources to schools to educate students to that level could perhaps be used nationally.

To ensure equitable resources across and among states would require the role of the federal government to be redefined as much more respon sible for and involved in state education systems and is quite unlikely. Issues of local control and federal budget constraints serve as strong im pediments for such a change to occur.

At present, the federal government can define general outputs of state education systems without being required to manage the input of re sources to those systems. In a June 25, 2009, decision of the U.S. Supreme Court on the *Horne v. Flores* (2009) case addressing inequity of funding to meet the learning needs of ELL students, the majority decision referred to a growing consensus in education research that increased funding alone does not improve student achievement without exploration of the other elements that, combined with funding, impact student achievement.

Any changes in the equity of school funding across states and among states appear to fall on the shoulders of state legislatures for the foresee able future as other factors related to student achievement are explored. As noted by the educators in this book, time and training for teachers to enact changes in the classroom require resources. While funding alone may not be the key to student achievement, it is difficult to imagine that how funding is used to support teachers and students does not have a dra matic impact on student achievement.

Political and Social Values

The reluctance to adequately fund all public schools begs the question of social values. If standards based education is indeed intended to leave no child behind and narrow the achievement gap among minority, poor, ELL, and special needs children to maximize America s human resource capital, what public investment is appropriate to support this effort?

Moral consciousness cannot be dictated, however, and, judging from past national political trends in education policy, it is not until the eco nomic welfare of those in power is threatened that the success of minority groups is viewed as essential or even relevant, such as in the economic downturn that produced the *Nation at Risk* report (National Commission on Excellence in Education 1983).

This is an admittedly cynical view and does not minimize the efforts of such educators as Darling Hammond (2010) and others to raise public awareness regarding resources needed to adequately and effectively edu cate all American children. It is simply the recognition that, at this time, the majority of society (as reflected by current public education policy) does not support allocating the resources needed to accomplish the goal of creating a standards led public education system that addresses both of the core tasks of schools: creating student centered learning environments and aligned curriculum, assessment, and instruction.

It can be done, however. Darling Hammond (2010) explains how three countries that have made substantive investments in their education sys tems have been catapulted . . . from the bottom to the top of international rankings in student achievement and attainment, graduating more than 90% of their young people from high school and sending large majorities through college (192).

She goes on to highlight common investments made by these countries, including the following:

- *Funded schools adequately and equitably* and added incentives for teaching in high need schools.
- *Revised national standards and curriculum* to focus on learning goals on higher order thinking, inquiry, and innovation as well as integration of technology throughout the curriculum. Teachers develop school based performance assessments to evaluate student learning, which in clude research projects, science investigations, and technology applica tions. Students are increasingly expected to learn to reflect on, evaluate, and manage their own learning.
- *Developed national teaching policies* that built strong teacher educa tion programs that recruit able students and completely subsidize their extensive training programs, paying them a stipend as they learn to teach well. Salaries are equitable across schools and competitive with other careers, generally comparable to those of engineers and other key professionals. Teachers are viewed as professionally prepared and well respected, and working conditions are supportive, including substantial participation in decision making about curriculum, instruction, assess ment, and professional development.
- *Supported ongoing teacher learning* by ensuring mentoring for beginning teachers and providing fifteen to twenty five hours a week for veteran teachers to plan collaboratively and engage in analyses of student learn ing, lesson study, action research, and observations of one another s classrooms that help them continually improve their practice. All three nations expect teachers to engage in research on practice, create incen tives for them to do so, and fund extensive ongoing professional develop ment opportunities in collaboration with universities and other schools.

Darling Hammond (2010) and Rothstein (2004) advocate for the incorpora tion of school visits to monitor and assess school effectiveness that is used in these other countries to support school reform and improvement as well.[1]

The key, perhaps, to the accomplishment of the previously mentioned reforms may rest in the management of education in these countries by professional ministries of education, which are substantially buffered from shifting political winds (2010, 193). It would require deft leader ship at the federal level to remove the U.S. Department of Education from the political arena and could be seen by many as contrary to the spirit of democratic policy development, if not rooted in the principles of Fourth Way change, as described by Hargreaves and Shirley (2009).

Based on the pillars of purpose, principles of professionalism, and cata lysts of coherence that have been identified as effective in building strong educational organizations and supportive educational policies in various countries, the Fourth Way can perhaps guide federal educational leaders in building support for the development of coherent educational policies and structures. The Fourth Way is described as promoting educational change through deepened and demanding learning, professional quality and engagement, and invigorated community development and public democracy (Hargreaves and Shirley 2009, 109).

The principles and purposes encompassed in the Fourth Way are highly compatible with and perhaps necessary for successful leadership of national implementation of standards led education as well as repre sentative of local leadership of the educational changes described in this book. These include an inspiring and inclusive vision, strong stakeholder engagement, investment in achievement, an active role for students, and mindful learning and teaching by all.

If other countries, such as those identified by Darling Hammond (2010), can create the necessary supportive structures and invest in public education in ways that increase the learning of all students, it is possible for America to do the same. Skilled nonpartisan discussion as to the true value placed on the educational opportunities and achievement of all students by American society is perhaps the key. Such a discussion can help to identify both the will and the means for enacting and supporting reforms, such as standards based educational practices, that can support the academic success of all students.

IMPLICATIONS FOR PRACTITIONERS
AND PREPARATION PROGRAMS

The role of district and school leaders in the implementation of standards based educational practices is vital. Just as district leaders must articulate the need for changes in the current system and allocate available resources to support the professional growth of principals and teachers who will carry out these changes, principals must also have a clear understanding of what a standards led system looks like in a classroom so that they can assist teachers with making the necessary instructional changes that are required.

Although the role of school leaders has perhaps not been identified as the key leadership position in enacting standards based change in the districts examined in this study, principals are responsible for articulating the values of a school through the supervision process and essential for nurturing the learning climate for both teachers and students (Waters et al. 2003). Educational leadership at both the district and the school level must engage in reflective dialogue to come to a common understanding of what standards led education looks like and how it can be accomplished.

Teachers, as well as educational leaders, must pursue professional growth and embrace a deprivatization of practice through collaboration. The topics listed earlier in this chapter can serve as a guide in this devel opmental process. These areas, when included in teacher and educational leadership preparation programs, can more fully prepare each for the roles they must assume in a standards led educational system.

No two educational settings are the same, and reforms and initiatives develop unique structures and consequences in response to the individu als, policies, and structures present in each particular setting. The leader ship actions of the administrators in the schools described in this book and the resulting learning of teachers, as well as changes in teachers practice, can be used as a guide or road map, however, by school and district lead ers who want to implement standards based instructional practices.

Much as teachers are expected to scaffold the learning of their students, administrators can scaffold the learning of teachers, identifying the cur rent knowledge and skill level of educators and the subsequent knowledge and skills that need to be developed, based on the stages explained in this book. Administrators can also assess the message and method of the vision they are articulating to faculty and other educational stakeholders based on the stages of implementation identified as well as how they are providing support to accomplish that vision.

Thinking about the goal and desired outcome of each step, each invest ment in professional development, and each message conveyed to others can help administrators clarify their beliefs about teaching and student achievement. This reflective process should make the change process more understandable and less intimidating. If leaders can clearly and consistently communicate the sequence and purpose of change, it is easier for those being asked to change to trust that the outcome is thoughtfully selected and the process for change is purposefully devised.

Preparation programs often expose preservice school and district lead ers to a variety of change theories, usually in very broad contexts. It is hoped that the change process described in this text can be used as a concrete example of long term and short term leadership decisions that exemplify effective change theories. Preparation programs can also assist preservice leaders in assessing the resources available to implement the changes in each stage as well as the venues and means of communicating the purpose for each change.

CONCLUSION

The value of having educational standards will continue to be debated, im pacted largely by the consequences that state and federal accountability sys tems place on various methods of assessing student learning of standards. The support for student learning of educational standards, as well as the ex pectations for performance and how performance is defined and measured, is an issue of public policy. While accountability for student performance on standardized state assessments provided the impetus for schools in this book to change many aspects of how instruction were delivered and as sessed, student learning and not just test scores became the focus of change in the later stages of standards based instructional implementation.

The bottom line for schools is helping students to learn the knowledge and skills that will help them to be successful adults who are capable and confident to make choices in life as well as active participants in society and the economy. Test scores and accountability systems provide discrete information and judgments on student learning. The responsibility to identify those relevant skills and knowledge needed by students, as well as how to structure the learning environment to support student learning, falls on the everyday actions of teachers and administrators in schools and districts, not policymakers.

It is hoped that the journeys described in this book can help educa
tors at all levels take responsibility for identifying desired educational
outcomes and making the decisions necessary to support student learn
ing. Leadership, creativity, reflection, and dialogue are required among
all education stakeholders for American schools to improve, as educa
tion is a shared social endeavor. Standards based education can be an
essential vehicle for improving schools but requires an investment in
adult learning first in order to support the learning and success of all
students.

The question that should guide the actions of educational leaders and
educators in the implementation of standards based educational practices,
as in all educational decisions, is, Does it change classroom instruction
and improve the learning opportunities and outcomes for all students?
If this question serves as the criteria for decision making by local, state,
and national educational leaders, significant changes in education policy,
support for schools, and the educational system are possible. The future of
public education depends on how educational leaders fulfill their respon
sibilities to students and society in the current context of standards based
education reform and accountability.

POINTS TO REMEMBER

- Education policy must support school reform.
- While fiscal resources alone will not change student achievement
  levels, how those resources are invested can positively impact student
  learning and success.
- Change is a learning process and requires support.
- Support for learning and change includes collaborative structures and
  professional development.
- Effective teaching is supported by collaborative professional develop
  ment, particularly in the area of assessment literacy.
- Educational leaders must invest in professional development in order
  to effectively implement standards based educational practices, change
  classroom learning environments, and support the achievement of all
  students.

NOTE

1. This structure of school visits and detailed feedback by educators to schools on the teaching and learning environment, student achievement, and community relations was implemented in Illinois in 1997. Although this quality assurance process was supported by school leaders and teachers as assisting school im provement efforts, an election brought new leadership to the state s education agency and a return to an emphasis on high standards, tough tests, and conse quential sanctions (Rau et al. 2002).

APPENDIXES

APPENDIX A

	Stages 1 and 2 of Standards-Based Education Implementation				
	Initial Alignment Stage		**Transitional Data Stage**		
	2–3 years		4–7 years		
Leadership Actions — Superintendent identifies a need for standards-based instruction	Superintendent enlists and empowers other district-level and/or building-level leaders to work with faculty on standards-based curriculum alignment		Identification and empowerment of an assessment coordinator/leader	Provision of standards-based professional development for teachers, internally or externally provided (teams, data analysis, rubrics, assessment of student learning)	
	Identification and empowerment of a curriculum coordinator/leader	Adoption of texts and other materials aligned with state standards	Implementation of district assessment system to complement state assessments but to provide more frequent, timely, and/or detailed feedback on student performance of state standards	Development or adoption of an online grade-reporting system	Development of a database correlating available student assessment data from state and district assessments
			Scheduling of collaborative team time by building-level leaders		
Teacher Actions	Curriculum back-mapping to align with learning standards		Identification of essential learning, "power standards," benchmarks		Initial identification of criteria for student demonstrations of proficiency on standards/benchmarks
	Attends informational sessions intended to create buy-in	In-service or collaborative time for faculty to align the curriculum with the state standards	In-services to share and analyze data	Team data analysis development	
			Attends assessment scoring workshops/trainings	Initial development of classroom assessment rubrics	
	Attends random workshops/in-service presentations on rudimentary concepts, goals, and practices scheduled by the district		Heavy reliance on textbook assessments and other materials adopted by the district that are aligned with the standards and approved as district curriculum		Begins sharing performance data with students

	Stages 3 and 4 of Standards-Based Education Implementation				
	Transitional Assessment Stage				Standards-Led Stage
	7–10 years			10–12 years	13–15 years
	Articulation of a redefinition of student achievement			Articulation of a redefinition of the role of school in student learning	
Leadership Actions	Implementation of standards-based student performance reporting of classroom assessments	Implementation of promotion to high school based on demonstration of standards competencies	Implementation of graduation standards based on demonstration of standards competencies	Implementation of grade promotion based on demonstration of standards competencies	Elimination of age-determined grade levels
		Refinement of criteria for student demonstration of proficiency to standards benchmarks			
Teacher Actions	Identification of criteria for student demonstration of proficiency to standards benchmarks	Begins articulation of rubrics/criteria of performance to students on classroom assessments	Begins articulation of the purpose of learning/standards to student		Purpose of learning/standards clearly articulated to students
	Continued development of classroom assessment rubrics	Begins to provide students with reassessment opportunities	Begins to listen to and/or solicit student input/choice in assessment methods	Begins to listen to and/or solicit student input into instructional methods	Student input is clearly evident and sought in instructional and assessment processes
	Continued sharing of performance data with students and collaborative goal setting	Begins using student performance data to guide (differentiation) instruction			Instruction guided by student performance assessment data
	Begins to provide students with preassessment or performance trial opportunities			Students have multiple opportunities and methods of demonstration competency of standards	
	Begins developing classroom assessments			Begins to seek student input on assessments	

APPENDIX B

Stage/Element	1 = Not Developed	2 = In Planning	3 = Partially Developed	4 = Being Refined	5 = Highly Developed
Stage 1: Initial Alignment					
Stage 1/1. District-led informational meetings with faculty regarding the need for and benefits of standards-based education (SBE)					
Stage 1/2. District-led informational meetings with parents, students, and community members regarding the need for and benefits of SBE					
Stage 1/3. Identification of a curriculum leader at the district level					
Stage 1/4. Alignment of local curriculum with state standards (correlation of grade and subject content with standards)					
Stage 1/5. Back-mapping of the local curriculum in alignment with state standards (teacher-generated outlines of content for each subject and grade level aligned with the standards, eliminating redundancy)					

Stage 1/6. Alignment of curricular materials with state standards			
Stage 1/7. Adoption of prealigned textbooks and supporting materials			
Stage 1/8. Documented utilization of aligned curriculum and materials in classroom			
Stage 1/9. Establishment of consistent and reoccurring collaboration time among teachers at grade level or by subject area			
Stage 1/10. Supportive involvement of administration in ongoing teacher collaboration efforts			
Stage 1/11. Professional development for alignment of curriculum			
Stage 1/12. Professional development for use of aligned curriculum			

continued

Stage/Element	1 = Not Developed	2 = In Planning	3 = Partially Developed	4 = Being Refined	5 = Highly Developed
Stage 1/13. Professional development for identification of student learning/products for specific standards/benchmarks					
Scores of 62–65 can be considered as having completed stage 1.					
Stage 2: Transitional Data					
Stage 2/1. Adoption of a district assessment system to provide more timely and detailed feedback on student performance of standards					
Stage 2/2. Regularly schedule time for teachers to examine data from state and district assessments					
Stage 2/3. Formation of grade and/or subject level teams					
Stage 2/4. Professional development on team effectiveness					
Stage 2/5. Professional development on data analysis					

Stage 2/6. Professional development on the effective classroom learning assessments			
Stage 2/7. Professional development on the development of rubrics			
Stage 2/8. Professional development on scoring student work			
Stage 2/9. Establishment of a district database to correlate student performance data			
Stage 2/10. District database includes an online grade-reporting system that is accessible by parents as well as teachers			
Stage 2/11. Teacher identification of essential learning associated with each standard			
Stage 2/12. Development of common classroom assessments by teachers			
Stage 2/13. Collaborative analysis of common classroom assessment data by teachers			

continued

Stage/Element	1 = Not Developed	2 = In Planning	3 = Partially Developed	4 = Being Refined	5 = Highly Developed
Stage 2/14. Identification of performance criteria for student demonstration of essential learning associated with each standard					
Stage 2/15. Teams adopt a norm of shared responsibility for student performance					
Scores of 72–75 on this section and a total score of 135–140 can be considered as having completed stage 2.					
Stage 3: Transitional Assessment					
Stage 3/1. District-led discussions with teachers regarding student achievement goals and assessment opportunities					
Stage 3/2. District-led discussions with parents, students, and community members regarding student achievement goals and assessment opportunities					
Stage 3/3. Development of a standards-based student performance reporting system at the elementary level					

Stage 3/4. Development of a standards-based student performance reporting system at the middle school level				
Stage 3/5. Development of a standards-based student performance reporting system at the high school level				
Stage 3/6. Development of a promotion system from elementary to middle school based on student demonstration of competency on state learning standards (key assessments)				
Stage 3/7. Development of a promotion system from middle to high school based on student demonstration of competency on state learning standards (key assessments)				
Stage 3/8. Development of a graduation system based on student demonstration of competency on state learning standards (key assessments or portfolio presentation)				

continued

Stage/Element	1 = Not Developed	2 = In Planning	3 = Partially Developed	4 = Being Refined	5 = Highly Developed
Stage 3/9. Teachers regularly (two to three times per week) articulate the criteria for student demonstration of proficiency on standards and/or benchmarks to students					
Stage 3/10. Almost all assignments/assessments are scored using rubrics that have been previously shared with students					
Stage 3/11. Teachers explain the purpose of the learning standard(s) addressed in each lesson and assessment to students					
Stage 3/12. Performance data are shared at least once a week with students					
Stage 3/13. Students help set performance targets with teachers					
Stage 3/14. Performance data are shared at least once a week among teacher team members and instructional strategies identified to respond to the data					

Stage 3/15. Teachers provide multiple assessment opportunities for major assessments					
Stage 3/16. Teachers provide preassessment or performance trials for major assessments					
Stage 3/17. Teachers use preassessment or performance trial data to establish a baseline for student performance and set learning goals					
Stage 3/18. Teachers use preassessment or performance trial data to establish a baseline for student performance, communicate learning expectations, and set learning goals with students					
Stage 3/19. Teachers solicit student input into assessment methods (i.e., rubric development, assessment options, etc.)					

continued

Stage/Element	1 = Not Developed	2 = In Planning	3 = Partially Developed	4 = Being Refined	5 = Highly Developed
Stage 4: Standards-Led					
Scores of 95–100 on this section and a total of 235–240 can be considered as having completed stage 3.					
Stage 4/1. District-led facilitation of discussion among teachers regarding the role of school in student learning					
Stage 4/2. District-led facilitation of discussion among parents, students, and community members regarding the role of school in student learning					
Stage 4/3. District-led facilitation of discussion among teachers regarding the structure/timing of student learning					
Stage 4/4. District-led facilitation of discussion among parents, students, and community members regarding the structure/timing of student learning					
Stage 4/5. Promotion is based on demonstration of competency of standards					

Stage 4/6. Age-based grade levels are eliminated				
Stage 4/7. Teachers solicit student input into instruction				
Stage 4/8. Student input is clearly evident in the instructional and assessment process				
Stage 4/9. Students have multiple opportunities and methods of demonstrating competency of the standards				
Stage 4/10. Students can articulate their learning progress				
Stage 4/11. Students can articulate their learning goals and associated learning strategies based on prior assessment data				

Scores of 52–55 on this section and a total score of 290–295 can be considered to have completed stage 4.

References

Ainsworth, L. 2003a. *Power standards: Identifying the standards that matter the most.* Englewood, CO: Advanced Learning Press.

———. 2003b. *Unwrapping the standards: A simple process to make standards manageable.* Englewood, CO: Advanced Learning Press.

Ainsworth, L., and J. Christinson. 1998. *Student generated rubrics: An assess ment model to help all students succeed.* Parsippany, NJ: Dale Seymour Pub lications.

Ainsworth, L., and D. Viegut. 2006. *Common formative assessments: How to connect standard based instruction and assessment.* Thousand Oaks, CA: Corwin Press.

Arter, J., and J. McTighe. 1998. *Scoring rubrics in the classroom: Using perfor mance criteria for assessing and improving student performance.* Thousand Oaks, CA: Corwin Press.

Baker, P. J., W. Rau, D. Ashby, A. Harper, and D. Floit. 2000. *Quality assur ance improvement planning pilot program: Third annual report.* Report to the Illinois State Board of Education. Illinois State University.

Berliner, D. C., and B. J. Biddle. 1996. *The manufactured crisis: Myths, frauds, and the attach on America s public schools.* 2nd ed. New York: Basic Books.

Blankstein, A. M. 2004. *Failure is not an option: Six principles that guide student achievement in high performing schools.* Thousand Oaks, CA: Corwin Press.

Bracey, G. W. 2004. *Setting the record straight: Responses to misconceptions about public education.* 2nd ed. Portsmouth, NH: Heinemann.

Brookhart, S. M. 2008. *How to give effective feedback to your students.* Alexan dria, VA: Association for Supervision and Curriculum Development.

Brookover, W. B., L. Beamer, H. Efthim, D. Hathaway, L. Lezotte, S. Miller, J. Passalacqua, and L. Tornatsky. 1982. *Creating effective schools: An inservice program for enhancing school learning climate and achievement.* Holmes Beach, FL: Learning Publications, Inc.

References

Bryk, A., and B. Schneider. 2002. *Trust in schools: A core resource for improve ment.* New York: Russell Sage Foundation.

Cavanagh, S. 2010. Resurgent debate, familiar theme: Common standards push bases unsettled issues. *Education Week Quality Counts* 2917: 5 11. Bethesda, MD: Editorial Projects in Education.

Comer, J. P. 2006. Our mission: It takes more than tests to prepare the young for success in life. *Education Week Quality Counts* 2517: 59 61. Bethesda, MD: Editorial Projects in Education.

Covington, M. V. 1993. *Making the grade: A self worth perspective on motiva tion and school reform.* New York: Cambridge University Press.

Crandall, D. 1982. *People, policies, and practice: Examining the chain of school improvement, V1 10.* Andover, MA: The Network.

Crandall, D., J. Eiseman, and K. S. Louis. 1986. Strategic planning issues that bear on the success of school improvement efforts. *Educational Administration Quarterly* 22, no. 2: 21 53.

Cuban, L. 2003. *Why is it so hard to get good schools?* New York: Teachers College Press.

Cunningham, W. G., and P. A. Cordeiro. 2003. *Educational leadership: A prob lem based approach.* 2nd ed. Boston: Allyn and Bacon.

Danzberger, J. P., M. W. Kirst, and M. D. Usdan. 1992. *Governing public schools: New times, new requirements.* Washington, DC: Institute for Educa tional Leadership.

Darling Hammond, L. 1997. *The right to learn: A blueprint for creating schools that work.* San Francisco: Jossey Bass.

———. 2010. *The flat world and education: How America s commitment to equity will determine our future.* New York: Teachers College Press.

DuFour, R., and R. Eaker. 1998. *Professional learning communities at work: Best practices for enhancing student achievement.* Alexandria, VA: Association for Supervision and Curriculum Development.

English, F. 2000. *Deciding what to teach and test: Developing, aligning, and auditing the curriculum.* Thousand Oaks, CA: Corwin Press.

Foorman, B. R., S. J. Kalinowski, and W. L. Sexton. 2007. Standards based educational reform is one important step toward reducing the achievement gap. In *Standards based reform and the poverty gap,* edited by A. Gamoran. Washington, DC: Brookings Institution Press.

Fox, T. 2009a. *Leading the way with standards based systems.* http://www.rfsd .k12.co.us/2009/02/leading the way with standards based systems.html#more.

———. 2009b. *Standards based grading What s in it for students?* http://www .rfsd.k12.co.us/2009/02/standards based grading whats in it for students.html.

. 2009c. *What s in a grade?* http://www.rfsd.k12.co.us/2009/02/whats in a grade.html#more.

Fullan, M. 1985. Change processes and strategies at the local level. *Elementary School Journal* 85, no. 3: 391 421.

. 1991. *The new meaning of educational change.* London: Cassell.

. 1993. *Change forces: probing the depths of educational reform.* New York: Falmer.

. 2001a. *Leading in a culture of change.* San Francisco: Jossey Bass.

. 2001b. *The new meaning of educational change.* 3rd ed. New York: Teachers College Press.

. 2005. *Leadership and sustainability: System thinkers in action.* Thousand Oaks, CA: Corwin Press.

Glickman, C. D. 1993. *Renewing America s schools: A guide for school based action.* San Francisco: Jossey Bass.

Glickman, C. D., S. P. Gordon, and J. M. Ross Gordon. 2009. *The basic guide to supervision and instructional leadership.* 2nd ed. New York: Allyn and Bacon.

Guskey, T. 2006. Making high school grades meaningful. *Phi Delta Kappan* 87, no. 9: 670 675.

Guthrie, J. W., and P. J. Schuermann. 2010. *Successful school leadership: Plan ning, politics, performance, and power.* Boston: Allyn and Bacon.

Hargreaves, A., and M. Fullan. 1998. *What s worth fighting for out there?* New York: Teachers College Press.

Hargreaves, A., and D. Shirley. 2009. *The fourth way: The inspiring future of educational change.* Thousand Oaks, CA: Corwin Press.

Hargreaves, D. H. 1984. *Improving secondary schools.* London: Inner London Education Authority.

Hightower, A. M. 2010. State of the states: Holding all states to high standards. *Education Week Quality Counts.* Vol. 2917. Bethesda, MD: Editorial Projects in Education.

Holcomb, E. L. 2009. *Asking the right questions: Tools for collaboration and school change.* Thousand Oaks, CA: Corwin Press.

Hord, S. M. 1997. *Professional learning communities: Communities of continu ous inquiry and improvement.* St. Newton, MA: Southwest Educational Devel opment Laboratory, U.S. Department of Education.

. 2007. *Leading professional learning communities: Voices from research and practice.* Thousand Oaks, CA: Corwin Press.

Huberman, M., and M. Miles. 1984. *Innovation up close.* New York: Plenum.

Joyce, B. 1993. *The self renewing school.* Alexandria, VA: Association for Su pervision and Curriculum Development.

Joyce, B., E. Calhoun, and D. Hopkins. 1999. *The new structure of school im provement: Inquiring schools and achieving students.* Philadelphia, PA: Open University Press.

Klimek, K. J., E. Ritzenehin, and K. D. Sullivan. 2008. *Generative leadership: Shaping new futures for today s schools.* Thousand Oaks, CA: Corwin Press.

Kohn, A. 1999. *The schools our children deserve: Moving beyond traditional classrooms and tougher standards.* New York: Houghton Mifflin.

———. 2010. Debunking the case for national standards. *Education Week Quality Counts.* Vol. 2917. Bethesda, MD: Editorial Projects in Education.

Kouzes, J. M., and B. Z. Posner. Z. 2007. *Leadership challenges.* 4th ed. San Francisco: Wiley.

Lortie, D. C. 1975. *Schoolteacher: A sociological study.* Chicago: University of Chicago Press.

Louis, K. S., and M. B. Miles. 1990. *Improving the urban high school: What works and why.* New York: Teachers College Press.

Matthews, L. J., and G. M. Crow. 2010. *The principalship: New roles in a profes sional learning community.* Boston: Allyn and Bacon.

Matthews, L. J., E. J. Williams, and G. M. Stewart. 2007. *Defining the elements of a learning community: A search of the existing literature.* Impact. Provo, UT: Utah Association of Secondary School Principals.

McMurrer, J. 2007. *Choices, changes, and challenges: Curriculum and instruc tion in the NCLB era.* Washington, DC: Center on Education Policy.

Meier, D. 2000. *Will standards save public education?* Boston: Beacon Press.

MetriTech. 2001. *Standards aligned classroom initiative survey.* Unpublished in strument. Bloomington, IL. Retrieved from http://www.isbe.state.il.us/board/ meetings/2000 2002/sept01meeting/SACIsurvyform.pdf.

Miller, L. S. 1995. *An American imperative: Accelerating minority educational advancement.* New Haven, CT: Yale University Press.

Miron, G., J. L. Urschel, J. L. Mathis, and E. Tornquist. 2010. *Schools without diversity: Education management organizations, charter schools, and the demographic stratification of the American school system.* Boulder, CO, and Tempe, AZ: Education and the Public Interest Center and Education Policy Research Unit. http://epicpolicy.org/publication/schools without diversity.

National Commission on Excellence in Education. 1983. *A nation at risk.* Washington, DC: U.S. Department of Education. http://www.ed.gov/pubs/Nat AtRisk/risk.html.

National Commission on Teaching and America s Future. 1996. *What matters most: Teaching for American s future.* New York: National Commission on Teaching and America s Future.

National Research Council. 2000. *How people learn: Brain, mind, experience, and school*. Washington, DC: National Academy Press.

———. 2001.*Knowing what students know: The science and design of educational assessment*. Washington, DC: National Academy Press.

Newmann, F. M., and Associates. 1996. *Authentic achievement: Restructuring schools for intellectual quality*. San Francisco: Jossey Bass.

Nichols, S. L., and D. C. Bracey. 2007. *Collateral damage: How high stakes testing corrupts America s schools*. Cambridge, MA: Harvard Education Press.

Noddings, N. 2010. Differentiate, don t standardize. *Education Week Quality Counts*. Vol. 2917. Bethesda, MD: Editorial Projects in Education.

Ohanian, S. 1999. *One size fits few: The folly of educational standards*. Portsmouth, NH: Heinemann.

Olson, L. 2006. A decade of effort. *Education Week Quality Counts*. Vol. 2517. Bethesda, MD: Editorial Projects in Education.

O Toole, J. 1995. *Leading change: Overcoming the ideology of comfort and the tyranny of custom*. San Francisco, CA: Jossey Bass.

Phillips, V., and C. Wong. 2010. Tying together the common core of standards, instruction, and assessments. *Phi Delta Kappan* 91, no. 5: 37 42.

Popham, W. J. 2003. *Test better, teach better: The instructional role of assessments*. Alexandria, VA: Association for Supervision and Curriculum Development.

———. 2010. *Classroom assessment: What teachers need to know*. 6th ed. Boston: Allyn and Bacon.

Purkey, S., and M. Smith. 1983. Effective schools. *Elementary School Journal* 83, no. 4: 427 52.

Rau, W., L. Vogel, P. Baker, and D. Ashby. 2002. *Inconstant activism and systemic errors by Illinois policy makers: An analysis of 15 years of educational policy zigzags*. Paper presented at the American Educational Research Association conference, New Orleans, LA, April 3.

Reeves, D. B. 2002. *The leader s guide to standards: A blueprint for educational equity and excellence*. San Francisco: Jossey Bass.

———. 2003. *Making standards work: How to implement standards based assessments in the classroom, school, and district*. Englewood, CO: Advanced Learning Press.

Reynolds, D. 1976. The delinquent school. In *The process of schooling*, edited by P. Woods. London: Routledge.

Rogers, S., J. Ludington, and S. Graham. 1997. *Motivation and learning: A teacher s guide to building excitement for learning and igniting the drive for quality*. Evergreen, CO: Peak Learning Systems, Inc.

Rosenholtz, S. J. 1991. *Teachers workplace: The social organization of schools.* New York: Teachers College Press.

Rost, J. C. 1991. *Leadership for the twenty first century.* Westport, CT: Praeger.

Rothstein, R. 2004. *Class and schools: Using social, economic, and educational reform to close the Black White achievement gap.* Washington, DC: Economic Policy Institute.

Rothstein, R., R. Jacobsen, and T. Wilder. 2008. *Grading education: Getting ac countability right.* Washington, DC: Economic Policy Institute.

Rutter, M., B. Maughan, P. Mortimore, and J. Ouston. 1979. *Fifteen thousand hours: Secondary schools and their effects on children.* Boston: Harvard University Press.

Sanchez Traynor, M. 2006. Pueblo district sets an example. *Greeley Tribune,* June 6. http://www.greeleytribune.com/article/20060604/SPECIALB1110/10 6040072&parentprofile=.

Sarason, S. B. 2002. *Educational reform: A self scrutinizing memoir.* New York: Teachers College Press.

Sawchuck, S. 2010. Teaching, curricular challenges looming. *Education Week Quality Counts.* Vol. 2917. Bethesda, MD: Editorial Projects in Education.

SBE Design Team. 1996. *Colorado standards based classroom self inventory.* Longmont, CO: Northern Colorado BOCES.

Schmoker, M. J. 2001. *Results fieldbook: Practical strategies from dramatically improved schools.* Alexandria, VA: Association for Supervision and Curriculum Development.

Sch n, D. 1984. *The reflective practitioner: How professionals think in action.* New York: Basic Books.

Senge, P. 2000. *Schools that learn: A fifth discipline fieldbook for educators, parents, and everyone who cares about education.* New York: Doubleday.

Sergiovanni, T. J. 1992. *Moral leadership: Getting to the heart of school im provement.* San Francisco: Jossey Bass.

Smith, S. C., and P. K. Piele. 2006. *School leadership: Handbook for excellence in student learning.* 4th ed. Thousand Oaks, CA: Corwin Press.

Sparks, D., and S. Hirsh. 2000. *A national plan for improving professional de velopment.* National Staff Development Council. http://www.nsdc.org/library/ NSDCPlan.html.

Stiggins, R. J. 2007. *Introduction to student involved assessment FOR learning.* 5th ed. Upper Saddle River, NJ: Pearson.

Stigler, J. W., and J. Hiebert. 1999. *The teaching gap: Best ideas from the world s teachers for improving education in the classroom.* New York: Free Press.

Tileston, D. W. 2004. *What every teacher should know about student assessment.* Thousand Oaks, CA: Corwin Press.

Tomlinson, C. A., and J. McTighe. 2006. *Integrating differentiated instruction and understanding by design.* Alexandria, VA: Association for the Supervision and Development of Curriculum.

Waters, T., R. J. Marzano, and B. McNulty. 2003. *Balanced leadership: What 30 years of research tells us about the effect of leadership on student achievement.* Denver: Mid Continent Research for Education and Learning.

Weick, K. 1976. Educational organizations as loosely coupled systems. *Adminis tration Science Quarterly* 21: 1 9.

Whitaker, T. 2010. *Leading school change: 9 strategies to bring everybody on board.* Larchmont, NY: Eye on Education.

Wiggins, G. 1998. *Educative assessment: Designing assessments to inform and improve student performance.* San Francisco: Jossey Bass.

Wiggins, G., and J. McTighe. 1998. *Understanding by design.* Alexandria, VA: Association for Supervision and Curriculum Development.

Wilson, B. C., and T. B. Corcoran. 1988. *Successful secondary schools.* London: Falmer.

Wolk, R. A. 2006. A second front: Betting everything on standards based reform is neither wise nor necessary. *Education Week Quality Counts* 2517. Bethesda, MD: Editorial Projects in Education.

Zemmelman, S., E. Daniels, and A. Hyde. 1998. *Best practice: New standards for teaching and learning in America s schools.* Portsmouth, NH: Heinemann.

About the Author

Linda R. Vogel is associate professor and program coordinator of educational leadership and policy studies at the University of Northern Colorado as well as the chair of the leadership development department. Dr. Vogel is a former junior high and high school teacher and principal.

In addition to her interest in standards based education reform and policy, she has conducted research in the areas of social justice perceptions of school leaders, school finance, and Native American educational leadership preparation. Dr. Vogel has directed several grant projects, including the Native American Innovative Leadership program at the University of Northern Colorado.